The Instant Pot® Electric Pressure Cooker Cookbook

THE INSTANT POT®
Electric Pressure Cooker
Cookbook

EASY RECIPES FOR FAST & HEALTHY MEALS

Laurel Randolph

ROCKRIDGE
PRESS

This book is dedicated to my husband, Dan,
for being the world's best recipe guinea pig.

~~~~~~

CONTENTS

INTRODUCTION

My love for pressure cooking runs deep. Some of my favorite childhood memories are of my grandmother's jiggle-top rattling away while she cooked a big pot of beans for dinner. I always tried to be in the kitchen when the beans were done cooking because I loved the intense steamy hiss when she opened the valve. Upon cracking open the lid, the house would fill with the smell of smoky pork, sweet onions, and spices. When it was time for me to set off for college, my grandmother sent me with her well-loved cooker. I made the occasional soup with the heavy pot, but it wasn't until I received an electric pressure cooker as a wedding gift that I fully realized the world of pressure-cooking possibilities. It had the same advantages of my grandmother's model without any of the guesswork—or all that racket. It opened my eyes to the sheer pleasure of cooking with pressure, and my cooker and I have been inseparable ever since.

In this book, we'll explore the surprising variety of easy dishes you can make with your electric pressure cooker. If you're lucky enough to own an Instant Pot, then you're probably aware of the many handy things this one inclusive device can do. But even Instant Pot enthusiasts may not realize just how much this cooker can achieve with the pressure-cooking setting alone. We'll explore a wide variety of dishes, from breakfast to dinner and stews to dessert, and use wholesome and healthy ingredients in the process. The vast majority of these recipes can be prepared in less than 45 minutes, and many are true one-pot meals, making meal planning and cleanup a cinch. Once you try these delicious dishes, you and your electric pressure cooker are sure to become inseparable, too.

CHAPTER ONE

FAST FOOD FOR GOOD HEALTH

Why use a pressure cooker? It all boils down to speed and versatility. By building up steam and, in turn, raising the pressure and temperature, pressure cookers can simulate the effects of long braises, boils, and simmers in no time at all. You save loads of cooking time and energy in the process without losing any of the taste and still maintaining texture.

This revolutionary form of cooking was invented in the late 1600s in the form of a large cast iron vessel with a lock top, and has continued to improve over the years. After a boom during and after WWII, pressure cooking saw a decline in popularity, until a recent resurgence. New and improved models, including the easy-to-use electric pressure cooker introduced in the '90s, have shown pressure cooking to be a safe, fast, and easy way to make nutritious and great-tasting meals.

Five Benefits of Pressure Cooking

There are lots of reasons to love pressure cooking, so treat the list of benefits below as just the beginning. As you expand your pressure cooking knowledge and experience, your list will only get longer.

› COOK FOOD FAST. Pressure cooking cuts traditional cooking times by up to 70 percent, making it great for super-quick meals. It greatly decreases typically long cooking times for dishes like beans, thick meats, and stocks, making slow weekend dishes into weekday options.

› PRESERVE NUTRITION FOR HEALTHY MEALS. Because pressure cooking requires less cooking liquid, it's more nutritious than boiling, as fewer minerals leach out of the food and into the liquid. The shorter cooking time also helps preserve the natural vitamins inside the food, making pressure cooking an exceptionally healthy cooking method.

› MAKE GREAT DISHES WITHOUT THE FUSS. Electric pressure cookers automatically regulate the pressure and use a timer to control the cooking time. These automated functions make them simpler to use than their stove-top counterparts, and their hands-off functionality make them extra safe and all-around user-friendly. This is an appliance you'll want to keep on your countertop.

› REDEFINE THE ONE-POT MEAL. In addition to greatly reducing cooking time, pressure cookers can turn out great-tasting one-pot meals. With little more to do than toss your ingredients in a pot and turn it on, meals don't get much easier than this. Make a hearty stew, healthy chili, or quick pasta dish in no time and with just one pot to clean.

› GO GREEN. With a faster cooking time and an efficient use of energy, pressure cookers are eco-friendly. When compared to stove-top and other cooking methods, pressure cooking uses two to three times less energy.

Step-by-Step Electric Pressure Cooking

The same thing that makes pressure cooking so great is what makes it intimidating: You drop in your ingredients, turn on the cooker, and let it go—no peeking allowed. The good news is we know enough about how food reacts under pressure to provide accurate cook times, removing all of the guesswork and allowing you to set it and forget it.

When it's time to get cooking, take a look at your chosen recipe. Does it involve browning or sautéing before pressure cooking? What is the pressure level, and how long is the cook time? Typical electric pressure-cooking recipes will involve the following steps, but read your recipe thoroughly before proceeding.

1. To enhance the flavor, use the Sauté function to sauté vegetables or brown meat before pressure cooking. Leave the top off when using this function.

2. Add the remaining ingredients and secure the lid with the steam release handle turned to the Sealing position.

3. Select the pressure level (High or Low) and cook time according to the recipe or manual. The cooker will automatically start.

4. Once pressure cooking is complete, turn off the cooker by selecting Cancel. This will disengage the warming function.

5. Use a natural release or quick release. A natural release, performed by selecting Cancel and letting the Instant Pot sit until the float valve sinks, slowly releases the pressure and locks in flavor. This can take

PRESSURE COOKING AT HIGH ALTITUDE

High-altitude cooking can be tricky, but pressure cookers provide an ideal method for preparing foods at high elevations. The efficient building of pressure overcomes many of the usual difficulties, making the appliance popular in high-altitude regions. Although the pressure is highly regulated inside the Instant Pot, the atmospheric pressure outside the cooker does affect cooking time. That means that if you live at high altitude, you will need to adjust the cook time called for in these (and other) recipes. The general rule is to add 5 percent to your cook time for every 1,000 feet above 2,000 feet elevation. For example, if you live at 3,000 feet, add 5 percent to your cook time. If you live at 5,000 feet and the recipe has a 20-minute cook time, add 15 percent to your cooking time, for a new cook time of 23 minutes.

10 minutes or more and is good for tough meats, stews, and sauces. Or release the steam manually for a quick release. Using extreme caution and a thick kitchen towel, turn the handle and quickly get out of the way while the steam releases for up to two minutes. This method is useful for delicate items with specific cooking times like vegetables or seafood.

6. Carefully remove the lid. Some dishes benefit from a simmer to help thicken, reduce, or concentrate the liquid. The Sauté function is handy again here, leaving you with just one dirty pot.

Using the Instant Pot Pressure Cooker

The Instant Pot is an all-in-one for fast and easy cooking, and once you get to know your cooker, the possibilities are endless. Give the manual that comes with the appliance a thorough read before using your Instant Pot, and continue to consult it as needed. You can find a downloadable manual at InstantPot.com/benefits/specifications-and-manuals.

The Instant Pot is composed of an exterior pot with a heating element inside and a control panel on the outside. The inner pot, which holds the food during cooking, sits snugly inside the exterior pot. The lid has a large handle and a steam release valve on top. The valve is used for a quick release, and must be in the Sealing position before pressure cooking can begin. Underneath the lid are a sealing ring, float valve, and exhaust valve. These are used to create a tight seal and regulate pressure within the Instant Pot.

The Instant Pot has a number of cooking functions. In this book, we will typically use the Manual function, with exceptions noted. With most functions, you can adjust the cook time or heat level using the Adjust, More (+), and Less (−) buttons. The Pressure key toggles between high and low pressure for all pressure-cooking functions except Rice. High pressure is the most common, and is used for most recipes; low pressure is for cooking delicate items like seafood. The Instant Pot will automatically begin preheating 10 seconds after the last key is pressed.

MANUAL The Manual setting is best used for pressure cooking when you want to input your settings from scratch. The recipes in this book tend to use the Manual function, and you can adjust the pressure and time as needed.

SAUTÉ The Sauté function is especially useful when preparing pressure cooker recipes since it allows you to perform multiple cooking methods in the same pot. We will use this function frequently to soften vegetables or brown meat before pressure cooking, as well as thicken sauces after pressure cooking. The low setting is best for slow simmering, normal is best for sautéing and browning, and high is best for charring or blackening. Safety tip: Leave the lid off when using this function.

SLOW COOK Slow cooking is a great option if you have a long, busy day ahead of you and want your dinner ready when you arrive home. Make sure the steam release handle is turned to the Venting position when using this function.

STEAM Designed for use with the included metal steam rack or your own appropriately sized steamer basket, the Steam function heats at full power continuously, boiling the water below and steaming the food in the basket.

BEAN/CHILI A function specifically for cooking dried beans at high pressure, the time can be adjusted for this function depending on how well cooked you like your beans.

MEAT/STEW This function can be used when cooking hearty meats at high pressure, and the time can be adjusted depending on which meats you use. Consult the Instant Pot manual or the Electric Pressure Cooking Time Charts in the back of this book when determining cook time.

MULTIGRAIN The Instant Pot makes cooking grains like wild and brown rice at high pressure quick and easy. Review the Instant Pot manual and consult the Electric Pressure Cooking Time Charts at the end of this book carefully when cooking grains, since the amount of liquid, cook time, and release are key to success.

PORRIDGE When using the Porridge function, the normal setting is for rice porridge, while the high setting is for a mixture of grains and beans. Use a natural release with this function.

POULTRY This automated function can be used for cooking chicken, turkey, or duck at high pressure. Consult the Instant Pot manual or the Electric Pressure Cooking Time Charts in the back of this book when determining cook time.

SAFETY TIPS FOR THE INSTANT POT

Every time you pressure-cook with your Instant Pot, keep a few safety tips in mind. Before each use, double-check that the bottom of your inner pot, as well as the heating plate that it sits on, are clean and dry. Check that the float valve, exhaust valve, and anti-block shield are also clean and free of any food, and make sure the sealing ring is secure. Finally, check that the steam release handle is in the Sealing position. When adding food, do not overfill the Instant Pot. Starchy foods or foods that are prone to foaming should not fill the pot more than half full. Other dishes should not fill the pot more than three-quarters full. After cooking is complete, remember that the cooker will be hot. Use extreme caution when releasing pressure, as steam can cause nasty burns if you're not careful. Use a thick kitchen towel or oven mitt to turn the handle and then quickly get out of the way. Always unplug your Instant Pot when not in use.

RICE This fully automated function is for cooking regular rice at low pressure, and the cooking duration is automatically adjusted based on the amount of rice and liquid in the cooker. You can cook as little as 1 cup of rice using this function.

SOUP Electric pressure cookers are excellent for making soups and broths, and this function keeps your soup from boiling too heavily.

YOGURT Homemade yogurt is made easy with this two-step Instant Pot function. See the Instant Pot manual for details.

The Instant Pot also has a Delayed Cooking function that further allows you to perfectly time your meals, as well as a Keep Warm feature. The warming feature is automatically activated once the cook timer runs out, and can be turned off by selecting Cancel. The pressure will release faster if you turn off the warming feature after cooking is complete. For all recipes in this book, select Cancel once pressure cooking is complete.

Converting Your Favorite Recipes

A wide range of dishes can be prepared in the pressure cooker, and once you've worked your way through the following recipes, you'll likely get the itch to convert a favorite slow cooker or stove-top dish to be pressure cooker–friendly. Most recipes can make the conversion easily as long as you keep a few things in mind.

› REDUCE THE AMOUNT OF LIQUID. Since pressure cookers don't allow evaporation like stove-top cooking, you don't need as much liquid. Adjust accordingly, but don't go under the minimum 1 cup of liquid.

› DECREASE THE COOK TIME. A dish cooked in a pressure cooker will typically take one-third to one-half of the cooking time of a traditional stove-top recipe. Compare your recipe and its ingredients to the cook time chart for best results.

› ADD DAIRY AT THE END. If the recipe includes dairy, the general rule is to add it at the end, after pressure cooking is over. Dairy tends to foam and scorch when heated in a pressure cooker. There are exceptions for certain recipes.

› THICKEN AT THE END. To thicken sauces or make a roux, use the Sauté function after pressure cooking. Thickeners like cornstarch and flour should be added after pressure cooking is over.

› DON'T OVERFILL. Pay attention to how big the recipe is and adjust so that you don't overfill your pot. Bigger recipes don't mean longer cook times, since the pressure cooker cooks everything at the same rate.

Try experimenting with a pressure-cooking converter like the one at HipPressureCooking.com/pressure-cooker-recipe-converter.

USING YOUR INSTANT POT PRESSURE COOKER

›	**DO double-check your pressure release handle.** If it's not in the Sealing position before you start pressure cooking, your Instant Pot won't have much success building enough pressure to properly cook the food.

›	**DO use the Sauté function and deglaze for extra flavor.** Browning aromatics and hearty meats before pressure cooking adds another layer of flavor. For sauces and stews with depth, deglaze the pan with wine, stock, or water.

›	**DO experiment.** Even though there are some don'ts when using a pressure cooker, once you learn the rules and become familiar with your machine, feel free to experiment!

›	**DO consult your manual on a regular basis.** Even longtime electric pressure-cooker users need to go back to their manual from time to time for assembly and troubleshooting info, recommended cook times, and more.

›	**DO make extra.** Most recipes for two to four people only fill the bottom quarter of the pot, so why not make extra? Most pressure-cooker recipes make great leftovers (like soups, grains, and beans) and even freeze well.

›	**DON'T use a quick release when cooking large amounts of some foods.** If you are making a big batch of soup or broth, use a natural release. Proceed with caution when cooking a large batch of gravy, noodles, whole grains, or porridge. These tend to foam, and if the Instant Pot is too full and you use a quick release, the handle can spray hot liquid.

›	**DON'T add too much liquid.** Pressure cookers trap steam, preventing the evaporation that occurs with stove-top cooking. This means you can cook with less liquid and achieve the same results while keeping the flavor concentrated. But don't go below the minimum amount, which is about 1 cup for the Instant Pot (depending on what you're cooking).

> › **DON'T use the cold water method.** Since we're cooking with electricity here, running the appliance under cold water for a quick release, as you would a stove-top pressure cooker, is a really bad idea.

> › **DON'T increase the cooking time when doubling a recipe.** Because the pressure cooks all of the food in the pot at the same rate, more food does not equal more cook time.

> › **DON'T overfill.** Even though you have a nice big pot, resist the temptation to fill it up. Never fill your Instant Pot over three-quarters full, and starchy and foamy dishes should only reach the halfway mark.

Cleaning and Caring for Your Electric Pressure Cooker

Keep your Instant Pot in good working order for years to come with a little TLC. After every use, unplug the Instant Pot and clean the inner pot with soapy water or wash it in the dishwasher. Clean the lid with a wet cloth and wipe dry. Remove the sealing ring and clean with soapy water when needed, and dry before replacing. The steam release valve can be removed for cleaning as well. Wipe the inside rim of the outer pot with a dry cloth.

When making strong-smelling dishes like curries and chilies, your sealing ring will take on these strong scents. Cleaning with warm, soapy water will help, and this typically won't affect the flavor of your food. If it bothers you, keep an extra ring around just for cooking aromatic foods.

If your Instant Pot produces unusual noises or burning smells, or if the power cord is damaged, immediately stop using it and unplug it. Contact customer support.

Regarding the Recipes

The recipes in this book are written to be easy to use and completely pain-free. Each states the prep time and pressure-cooking time along with the total time, which includes prep, cook, preheat, *and* de-pressurize time—giving you a true picture of how long the recipe will take from start to finish. Servings, settings used, and helpful tips like using a smart program, ingredient info, and substitutions are also included. Note that the heat settings labeled More and Less on the Instant Pot are referred to as High and Low in this book. If a heat setting is not specified, then leave as Normal—the automatic setting.

The recipes are also clearly marked with labels to make them easy to pick and choose:

› VIRTUALLY INSTANT recipes are ready in 20 minutes or less.

› WEEKDAY WIN recipes indicate complete meals that are done in 45 minutes or less.

› WORTH THE WAIT recipes take 1 hour or longer from start to finish, but their delicious results make up for the extra effort required.

› FAMILY-FRIENDLY recipes use kid-friendly ingredients and serve four or more.

Vegetarian, gluten-free, and Paleo-friendly recipes are also labeled.

HOLIDAY PRESSURE COOKING

Free up your oven for food-centric holidays with the help of the Instant Pot!

St. Patrick's Day
Corned Beef: page 114
Horseradish Mashed
    Potatoes: page 48
Braised Cabbage: page 42

**Memorial Day, Fourth of July,
and Labor Day**
Baby Back Ribs: page 118
Pulled Pork: page 119
Low-Country Boil: page 90
Charred Corn on the Cob: page 39

Jewish Holidays
One-Hour Matzo Ball Soup: page 75
Barbecue Beef Brisket: page 111
White Wine–Poached Pears with
    Vanilla: page 136

Thanksgiving and Christmas
Stuffed Turkey Breast: page 104
Rustic Herb Stuffing: page 65
Cranberry Sauce: page 151
Onion Gravy: page 149
Sweet Potatoes with Brown Sugar
    Topping: page 49
Little Pumpkin Puddings: page 130

BREAKFAST

Apple and Cinnamon Oatmeal

VEGETARIAN, GLUTEN-FREE *Heart-healthy steel-cut oatmeal cooks up perfectly in no time in the pressure cooker, and cinnamon and apple make this an autumn morning must. If you've never tried steel-cut oats, they're instant oats' chewier, healthier cousin. If you're gluten-intolerant, be sure to buy oats that are labeled as gluten-free. Top with chopped walnuts for a bit of protein.*

PREP: 5 MINUTES • PRESSURE: 7 MINUTES • TOTAL: 30 MINUTES
PRESSURE LEVEL: HIGH • RELEASE: NATURAL

SERVES 4

3 tablespoons butter

1 cup steel-cut oats

2½ cups water

1 large apple, cored, peeled, and chopped, plus more for garnish

1 tablespoon brown sugar, plus extra for serving

1 teaspoon ground cinnamon

¼ teaspoon kosher salt

1. To preheat the Instant Pot, select Sauté.

2. Once hot, add the butter and melt. Add the oats and stir, cooking for 2 minutes.

3. Add the water, apple, brown sugar, cinnamon, and salt and stir. Secure the lid.

4. Select Manual and cook at high pressure for 7 minutes.

5. Once cooking is complete, use a natural release for 10 minutes, then release any remaining pressure. The oatmeal will continue to thicken as it cools.

6. Serve the oatmeal topped with chopped fresh apple and more brown sugar.

VARIATION TIP: To make this recipe even more apple-y, replace up to 1 cup of the water with apple cider and omit the sugar.

Per Serving Calories: 243; Total Carbohydrates: 30g; Saturated Fat: 6g; Trans Fat: 0g; Fiber: 4g; Protein: 6g; Sodium: 209mg

Savory Breakfast Porridge

Not all breakfast porridge has to be sweet. Quite to the contrary, rice porridge, or congee, is a popular savory breakfast in China, and for good reason. It's creamy and nourishing without the need for dairy, and topped with a fried egg and soy sauce, it's also a delicious way to start the day.

PREP: 5 MINUTES • PRESSURE: 30 MINUTES • TOTAL: 1 HOUR
PRESSURE LEVEL: HIGH • RELEASE: NATURAL

SERVES 4

½ cup long-grain white rice, rinsed and drained

2 cups chicken broth

2 cups water

1 tablespoon sugar

½ teaspoon kosher salt, plus more for seasoning

1 tablespoon extra-virgin olive oil

4 eggs

Freshly ground black pepper

4 scallions, chopped

2 teaspoons soy sauce, plus more if needed

Chili sauce (optional)

1. Add the rice, broth, water, sugar, and salt to the Instant Pot and stir. Secure the lid.

2. Select Porridge and cook at high pressure for 30 minutes.

3. Meanwhile, heat the oil over medium heat in a large skillet or frying pan (preferably nonstick). Once hot, crack the eggs into the pan, next to each other but without touching. Cook, covered for half of the time, for 3 to 5 minutes, or until the whites are crispy and the yolks are still runny. Season with salt and pepper.

4. Once pressure cooking is complete, use a natural release. This will take about 15 minutes.

5. If you want a thicker porridge, select Sauté and simmer for up to 10 minutes.

6. Serve topped with scallions, soy sauce, chili sauce (if using), and an egg. Season with additional salt and pepper as desired.

VARIATION TIP: Porridge can be made with brown rice. Adjust the pressure cooking time to 45 minutes.

Per Serving Calories: 214; Total Carbohydrates: 24g; Saturated Fat: 2g; Trans Fat: 0g; Fiber: 1g; Protein: 10g; Sodium: 887mg

Cinnamon-Raisin French Toast Bake

VEGETARIAN *If you prefer your French toast hands-off, throw together this casserole for breakfast or brunch. It's a handy way to use up old bread, and has all the flavor and texture of French toast plus a little cinnamon spice. If you want a crisp top, sprinkle with sugar and slide under the broiler for a few minutes at the end.*

PREP: 10 MINUTES • PRESSURE: 15 MINUTES • TOTAL: 35 MINUTES
PRESSURE LEVEL: HIGH • RELEASE: QUICK

SERVES 4

1½ cups water

1 teaspoon butter

3 large eggs, beaten

1 cup whole or 2 percent milk

2 tablespoons maple syrup, plus more for serving

1 teaspoon vanilla extract

3 cups stale or lightly toasted cinnamon-raisin bread, cut into ¾-inch cubes

1 teaspoon sugar (optional)

1. Prepare the Instant Pot by adding the water to the pot and placing the steam rack on top.

2. Butter a 6- to 7-inch soufflé or baking pan. (If your dish doesn't have handles, make a sling for it before putting it into the pot. See the Cooking Tip for instructions.)

3. In a large bowl, whisk together the eggs, milk, maple syrup, and vanilla. Add the bread and let it sit for 5 minutes, stirring once or twice.

4. Pour the mixture into the pan and push down to submerge the bread, if needed. Place the dish on the steam rack, uncovered, and secure the lid.

5. Select Manual and cook at high pressure for 15 minutes.

6. Once cooking is complete, use a quick release. Be sure to remove the lid carefully and quickly so that condensation doesn't drip on the French toast.

7. Carefully remove the pan using a sling or handles. If a crispy top is desired, sprinkle with sugar and broil for 3 to 5 minutes.

COOKING TIP: A 6- or 7-inch baking pan or soufflé dish will come in handy when making a variety of dishes in your Instant Pot. If your dish or steam rack doesn't have handles, create a sling with a piece of aluminum foil, folded in half twice, that's long enough to go under the dish and stick up 6 inches on each side, creating "handles."

VARIATION TIP: This recipe tastes great with a topping of tangy yogurt.

Per Serving Calories: 183; Total Carbohydrates: 21g; Saturated Fat: 3g; Trans Fat: 0g; Fiber: 0g; Protein: 8g; Sodium: 172mg

Soft-Boiled Eggs and Soldiers

VEGETARIAN *Kids and adults alike will love spending their morning dipping toast "soldiers" into runny egg yolks. The Instant Pot produces perfect soft-boiled eggs every time, and while they steam, you can toast and cut your bread. Breakfast is ready in 15 minutes flat.*

PREP: 5 MINUTES • PRESSURE: 6 MINUTES • TOTAL: 15 MINUTES
PRESSURE LEVEL: LOW • RELEASE: QUICK

SERVES 4

1 cup water

4 eggs

1 to 2 tablespoons butter

4 to 8 bread slices

1. Prepare the Instant Pot by adding the water to the pot and placing the steam rack on top.

2. Place the eggs on the steam rack and secure the lid.

3. Select Manual and cook at low pressure for 6 minutes.

4. While the eggs cook, butter and toast the bread. Cut into 1-inch strips.

5. Once cooking is complete, use a quick release. Carefully remove the eggs and place in egg cups.

6. Use a spoon to tap around the top of the egg in a circle. Remove the top circle of shell and the section of egg along with it, exposing the runny yolk.

7. Serve with the toast for dunking.

DID YOU KNOW? Eggs and soldiers is a popular British breakfast, and the toast is often spread with Marmite or, in Australia, Vegemite.

Per Serving Calories: 162; Total Carbohydrates: 9g; Saturated Fat: 5g; Trans Fat: 0g; Fiber: 0g; Protein: 7g; Sodium: 225mg

Bacon and Egg Strata

A breakfast all-in-one, this strata combines bread, eggs, cheese, and bacon into one simple but tasty dish. It's an ingenious way to use up stale bread, and the texture is similar to bread pudding. Top it with cheese and broil it at the end for a crispy top.

FAMILY-FRIENDLY

PREP: 15 MINUTES • PRESSURE: 15 MINUTES • TOTAL: 45 MINUTES
PRESSURE LEVEL: HIGH • RELEASE: NATURAL

SERVES 4 TO 5

4 bacon slices

1½ cups water

1 tablespoon butter

3 large eggs, beaten

1 cup whole or 2 percent milk

Kosher salt

Freshly ground black pepper

3 cups stale whole-wheat bread, cut into ¾-inch cubes

¼ cup shredded sharp Cheddar cheese, plus 2 tablespoons for topping

1. In a sauté or frying pan over medium-high heat, crisp the bacon on both sides and place on a paper towel to drain. When cool enough, cut the bacon into small pieces.

2. Prepare the Instant Pot by adding the water to the pot and placing the steam rack on top.

3. Butter a 6- to 7-inch soufflé or baking dish. (If your dish doesn't have handles, make a sling for it before putting it into the pot. See the Cooking Tip for instructions.)

4. In a large bowl, whisk together the eggs and milk and season with salt and pepper. Add the bread and let it sit for 5 minutes, stirring once or twice.

5. Add ¼ cup of cheese and the bacon to the bowl and mix. Pour into the pan and push down to submerge, if needed. Place the dish on the steam rack, uncovered, and secure the lid.

6. Select Manual and cook at high pressure for 15 minutes.

7. Once cooking is complete, use a natural release. Be sure to remove the lid carefully and quickly so that condensation doesn't drip on the strata. ▶

Bacon and Egg Strata (continued)

8. Carefully remove the pan using oven mitts or tongs.

9. Preheat the oven to broil.

10. Top with the remaining 2 tablespoons of cheese and place under the broiler for 3 to 5 minutes until melted and browned.

COOKING TIP: A 6- or 7-inch baking pan or soufflé dish will come in handy when making a variety of dishes in your Instant Pot. If your dish or steam rack doesn't have handles, create a sling with a piece of foil, folded in half twice, that's long enough to go under the dish and stick up 6 inches on each side, creating "handles."

VARIATION TIP: Try adding a handful of finely chopped onion and bell pepper.

Per Serving Calories: 321; Total Carbohydrates: 12g; Saturated Fat: 10g; Trans Fat: 0g; Fiber: 1g; Protein: 20g; Sodium: 766mg

Sausage and Cheese Frittata

GLUTEN-FREE *Sausage, egg, and cheese are all cooked together in this fluffy frittata for a savory breakfast. You can always swap out the sausage for a few strips of bacon, or toss in diced onion and pepper. If you have two 6- to 7-inch baking dishes, double the recipe and stack the dishes on top of each other to serve more people.*

PREP: 15 MINUTES • PRESSURE: 17 MINUTES • TOTAL: 40 MINUTES
PRESSURE LEVEL: LOW • RELEASE: QUICK

SERVES 2 TO 4

1½ cups water

1 tablespoon butter

4 eggs, beaten

2 tablespoons sour cream

½ cup crumbled, cooked sausage

¼ cup grated Cheddar cheese

Kosher salt

Freshly ground black pepper

1. Add the water to the empty Instant Pot and place the steam rack on top.

2. Butter a 6- to 7-inch soufflé or baking dish. (If your dish doesn't have handles, make a sling for it before putting it into the pot. See the Cooking Tip for instructions.)

3. In a medium bowl, beat together the eggs and sour cream. Add the sausage and cheese and mix. Season with salt and pepper.

4. Pour the mixture into the buttered pan. Cover with foil and place on the steam rack. Secure the lid.

5. Select Manual and cook at low pressure for 17 minutes.

6. Once cooking is complete, use a quick release. Very carefully remove the pan.

7. If desired, broil for a few minutes for a browned top.

COOKING TIP: A 6- or 7-inch baking pan or soufflé dish will come in handy when making a variety of dishes in your Instant Pot. If your dish doesn't have handles, create a sling with a piece of foil, folded in half twice, that's long enough to go under the dish and stick up 6 inches on each side, creating "handles."

VARIATION TIP: Swap out the sausage for bacon, or go meatless with vegan sausage. Toss in some finely chopped onion and pepper for a western omelet-style frittata.

Per Serving Calories: 282; Total Carbohydrates: 1g; Saturated Fat: 12g; Trans Fat: 0g; Fiber: 0g; Protein: 16g; Sodium: 385mg

Potato and Pepper Frittata

VEGETARIAN , GLUTEN-FREE *Potatoes, peppers, and onions fill out this satisfying frittata, and a sprinkling of cheese makes it family friendly. You can double the recipe by using two baking dishes stacked on top of each other.*

PREP: 15 MINUTES • PRESSURE: 17 MINUTES • TOTAL: 40 MINUTES
PRESSURE LEVEL: LOW • RELEASE: QUICK

SERVES 2 TO 4

1½ tablespoons extra-virgin olive oil

1 large or 2 medium red or yellow potatoes, cut into ¼-inch slices

½ onion, cut into ⅛-inch slices

½ red bell pepper, seeded and cut into ¼-inch rings

1½ cups water

Butter, for greasing

4 eggs, beaten

2 tablespoons sour cream

Kosher salt

Freshly ground black pepper

¼ cup grated Monterey Jack or Cheddar cheese

1. Preheat the Instant Pot by selecting Sauté. Add the oil. Once hot, add the potatoes in one layer. Cook for 4 minutes, flip, and cook on the other side for 2 minutes. Remove.

2. Add the onion and cook for 2 minutes. Add the bell pepper and cook for 2 minutes more, until the onion is translucent. Remove from the pot. Select Cancel.

3. Add the water to the empty pot and place a steam rack on top. Butter a 6- or 7-inch round soufflé or baking dish.

4. In a medium bowl, beat together the eggs and sour cream. Season with salt and pepper.

5. Layer half of the potatoes, onion, and bell pepper in the baking dish and season with salt and pepper. Pour half of the egg mixture over the vegetables and sprinkle with half of the cheese. Repeat, ending with cheese.

6. Cover with foil and place on the steam rack. Secure the lid.

7. Select Manual and cook at low pressure for 17 minutes.

8. Once cooking is complete, use a quick release. Carefully remove the baking dish. If desired, broil in the oven for a few minutes for a browned top.

COOKING TIP: If your dish doesn't have handles, create a sling with a piece of foil, folded twice, that's long enough to go under the dish and stick up 6 inches on each side, creating "handles."

Per Serving Calories: 470; Total Carbohydrates: 38g; Saturated Fat: 10g; Trans Fat: 0g; Fiber: 5g; Protein: 19g; Sodium: 315mg

Eggs in Purgatory with Eggplant

VEGETARIAN *The name of this dish comes from the spicy red tomato sauce that cooks the eggs. The combination of the bright sauce, soft eggplant, and rich eggs is fitting for brunch, lunch, or dinner. Serve with enough crusty bread for dunking.*

PREP: 30 MINUTES • PRESSURE: 10 MINUTES • TOTAL: 50 MINUTES
PRESSURE LEVEL: HIGH • RELEASE: QUICK

SERVES 2 TO 4

1 small eggplant, mostly peeled, cut into ½-inch pieces

1 tablespoon kosher salt, plus more for seasoning

2 tablespoons extra-virgin olive oil

3 large garlic cloves, minced

1 (28-ounce) can crushed tomatoes, with most of the liquid drained out

1 tablespoon harissa or 1 teaspoon smoked paprika

¼ teaspoon red pepper flakes

Freshly ground black pepper

4 to 6 eggs

1 tablespoon chopped fresh parsley

4 to 6 thick slices good-quality rustic bread, for serving

Hot sauce, for serving (optional)

1. In a large bowl, toss the eggplant with the salt and spread out onto a paper towel–lined baking sheet. Let it sit for 15 to 30 minutes. Take more paper towels and press out any moisture, wiping away some of the salt as you go.

2. Preheat the Instant Pot by selecting Sauté.

3. Once hot, add the oil. Add the eggplant and cook, stirring and scraping the bottom of the pot, for 4 minutes, until the eggplant is starting to cook. Add the garlic and cook for 1 minute more.

4. Add the tomatoes, harissa or paprika, and red pepper flakes, and season with black pepper. Secure the lid.

5. Select Manual and cook at high pressure for 10 minutes.

6. Once cooking is complete, use a quick release. Select Sauté and stir the sauce. Crack the eggs, one at a time, into a small bowl and lower each one into the pot, laying it on top of the sauce.

7. Cook, loosely covered, until the eggs are set but the yolks are still runny, 4 to 6 minutes.

8. Top with parsley and serve with bread and hot sauce (if using).

INGREDIENT TIP: Harissa is a North African hot chili pepper paste, and can be found in the international section of the grocery store or at Middle Eastern markets.

Per Serving Calories: 680; Total Carbohydrates: 87g; Saturated Fat: 5g; Trans Fat: 0g; Fiber: 23g; Protein: 31g; Sodium: 1688mg

CHAPTER THREE
VEGETABLES

Steamed Artichokes with Dipping Sauce

VEGETARIAN, GLUTEN-FREE *Artichokes are a vegetable that I wouldn't touch without the help of my pressure cooker. The tough, flowery vegetables are made tender and succulent in no time, and a zesty dipping sauce makes them a fun appetizer.*

PREP: 5 MINUTES • PRESSURE: 11–14 MINUTES • TOTAL: 30 MINUTES
PRESSURE LEVEL: HIGH • RELEASE: NATURAL

SERVES 2 TO 4

2 large artichokes

1 lemon, halved

1 cup water

3 tablespoons mayonnaise

1 teaspoon Dijon mustard

Pinch smoked paprika

1. Remove the damaged outer leaves of the artichokes. Trim the bottoms to be flat so that they sit up straight. Trim the tough ends of the leaves and rub with 1 lemon half.

2. Pour the water into the Instant Pot and insert a steamer basket. Place the artichokes in the basket sitting up (bloom facing up).

3. Secure the lid and select Manual. Cook at high pressure for 11 to 14 minutes depending on the size of your artichokes (the bigger the artichoke, the longer the cook time).

4. Once cooking is complete, use a natural release. Test the artichokes for doneness. If they aren't tender enough, continue to cook for a few minutes more.

5. In a medium bowl, mix together the mayonnaise, mustard, paprika, and a generous squeeze of lemon juice. Serve the artichokes warm with the dipping sauce on the side.

COOKING TIP: A steamer basket is a worthy investment when cooking with a pressure cooker. Look for one with sturdy legs and a handle for retrieving from the pot. Double-check that it will fit in your Instant Pot, too.

Per Serving Calories: 173; Total Carbohydrates: 25g; Saturated Fat: 1g; Trans Fat: 0g; Fiber: 10g; Protein: 6g; Sodium: 338mg

Eggplant and Roasted Red Pepper Dip

VEGETARIAN, GLUTEN-FREE, PALEO-FRIENDLY *Eggplant and roasted red peppers are magically transformed into a creamy dip that's healthy, too. It's similar to baba ganoush, but not as smoky. What it lacks in smokiness it makes up for in texture and flavor.*

PREP: 10 MINUTES • PRESSURE: 3 MINUTES • TOTAL: 20 MINUTES
PRESSURE LEVEL: HIGH • RELEASE: QUICK

SERVES 6 TO 8

5 tablespoons extra-virgin olive oil, divided

2 pounds eggplant, at least half peeled but leaving some skin, and cut into 1-inch chunks

4 garlic cloves, minced

1 cup water

1 teaspoon kosher salt

¾ cup roasted red peppers, chopped

3 tablespoons freshly squeezed lemon juice

1 tablespoon tahini

1 teaspoon ground cumin

Freshly ground black pepper

1. To preheat the Instant Pot, select Sauté.

2. Once hot, add 3 tablespoons of oil. Add half of the eggplant and let brown on one side for 4 to 5 minutes. Remove and add another 1 tablespoon of oil to the pot, followed by the garlic and the remaining eggplant. Cook for 1 minute. Return the first batch of eggplant to the pot, and add the water and salt. Secure the lid.

3. Select Manual and cook at high pressure for 3 minutes.

4. Once cooking is complete, use a quick release. Add the roasted red peppers and stir. Let it sit for 5 minutes.

5. Carefully drain out most of the cooking liquid. Add the remaining 1 tablespoon of oil, lemon juice, tahini, and cumin and season with pepper.

6. Use an immersion blender to blend until smooth. Alternatively, purée in a blender in batches. Taste for seasoning. Serve with bread or pita for dipping.

INGREDIENT TIP: You can make your own roasted red peppers. Place whole red bell peppers in a preheated 450°F oven for 40 minutes. Cover with foil and let them sit for 30 minutes. Peel, stem, and seed the peppers before chopping them.

Per Serving Calories: 165; Total Carbohydrates: 12g; Saturated Fat: 2g; Trans Fat: 0g; Fiber: 6g; Protein: 3g; Sodium: 451mg

Steamed Edamame with Garlic

VEGETARIAN *Edamame, also known as fresh soybeans, are a tasty snack that happens to be high in fiber and nutrients. Serve them in their pods sprinkled with sea salt or covered in garlic for a fun, guilt-free appetizer.*

PREP: 5 MINUTES • PRESSURE: 3 MINUTES • TOTAL: 15 MINUTES
PRESSURE LEVEL: HIGH • RELEASE: QUICK

SERVES 4 TO 6

1 cup water

2 cups fresh or frozen edamame, in their pods

1 teaspoon sesame oil or extra-virgin olive oil

3 large garlic cloves, minced

1 tablespoon soy sauce

Sea salt

1. Add the water to the Instant Pot and place a steamer basket on top. Add the edamame and secure the lid.

2. Select Steam and cook at high pressure for 3 minutes.

3. Meanwhile, in a small sauté pan over medium heat on the stove, add the oil. Once hot, add the garlic and sauté for 1 to 2 minutes, until cooked but not brown. Add the soy sauce and turn off the heat.

4. Once pressure cooking is complete, use a quick release. Carefully remove the steamer basket. In a medium bowl, toss the edamame with the garlic mixture. Sprinkle with salt.

INGREDIENT TIP: Edamame can commonly be found in the frozen vegetables section of the supermarket. Buy the uncooked pods.

Per Serving Calories: 105; Total Carbohydrates: 8g; Saturated Fat: 1g; Trans Fat: 0g; Fiber: 2g; Protein: 8g; Sodium: 292mg

Easy Egg Salad

VEGETARIAN, GLUTEN-FREE *For the best, easy-to-peel cooked eggs, steaming is the way to go. With the help of a steam rack and the low pressure function on the Instant Pot, you'll have perfect boiled eggs every time. And what better to do with boiled eggs than make egg salad? Serve on top of a salad, as a sandwich, or with crackers.*

PREP: 7 MINUTES • PRESSURE: 7 MINUTES • TOTAL: 20 MINUTES
PRESSURE LEVEL: LOW • RELEASE: QUICK

SERVES 3 TO 4

1 cup water

6 eggs

⅓ cup finely diced celery

¼ cup high-quality or homemade mayonnaise

2 teaspoons minced fresh parsley

1 teaspoon Dijon or whole-grain mustard

1 teaspoon freshly squeezed lemon juice

Kosher salt

Freshly ground black pepper

1. Prepare the Instant Pot by adding the water to the pot and placing the steam rack on top.

2. Place the eggs on the steam rack and secure the lid.

3. Select Manual and cook at low pressure for 7 minutes.

4. While the eggs cook, add the celery, mayonnaise, parsley, mustard, lemon juice, and a sprinkle of salt and pepper to a medium bowl. Stir to combine.

5. Once cooking is complete, use a quick release. Let the eggs cool for 30 seconds and then rinse under cold water until cool.

6. Peel the eggs and add to the bowl. Mash with a fork for the desired consistency and mix with the mayonnaise mixture.

7. Store in an airtight container in the refrigerator for up to 3 days.

VARIATION TIP: I like my yolks solid but creamy for egg salad. If you like your yolks well done, add 1 minute to the cooking time.

Per Serving Calories: 208; Total Carbohydrates: 6g; Saturated Fat: 4g; Trans Fat: 0g; Fiber: 0g; Protein: 12g; Sodium: 356mg

Quick Zucchini Ratatouille

VEGETARIAN, GLUTEN-FREE, PALEO-FRIENDLY *Ratatouille is a classic French dish of fresh summertime vegetables (as seen in the beloved animated film of the same name). This recipe omits the usual eggplant, replacing it with extra zucchini, and is ready in 20 minutes flat. Serve with pasta, rice, or crusty bread.*

PREP: 5 MINUTES • PRESSURE: 3 MINUTES • TOTAL: 20 MINUTES
PRESSURE LEVEL: HIGH • RELEASE: QUICK

SERVES 4

1 tablespoon extra-virgin olive oil, plus extra for serving

1 medium yellow onion, finely chopped

1 large red bell pepper, finely chopped

2 garlic cloves, minced

4 medium zucchini, chopped into bite-size pieces

¼ cup dry white wine

2 large tomatoes, seeded and diced, or 2 handfuls large cherry tomatoes, halved

1 bay leaf

3 fresh thyme sprigs

Kosher salt

Freshly ground black pepper

2 tablespoons torn fresh basil

1. To preheat the Instant Pot, select Sauté on high heat.

2. Once hot, add the oil followed by the onion, bell pepper, and garlic. Cook, stirring occasionally, for 2 minutes or until the vegetables start to brown.

3. Add the zucchini and stir, cooking for about 3 minutes until the zucchini starts to brown. Add the wine and use a wooden spoon to scrape any brown bits from the bottom of the pot.

4. Add the tomatoes, bay leaf, and thyme and season with salt and pepper.

5. Secure the lid, select Manual, and cook at high pressure for 3 minutes.

6. Once cooking is complete, use a quick release. Select Sauté on high heat and cook for 2 to 3 minutes more to reduce the liquid.

7. Remove the bay leaf. Let the ratatouille cool for a few minutes before plating and topping with fresh basil and a drizzle of olive oil.

VARIATION TIP: If you're not eating vegan, this dish tastes great with freshly grated Parmesan on top. Replace the wine with broth, if desired.

Per Serving Calories: 111; Total Carbohydrates: 15g; Saturated Fat: 1g; Trans Fat: 0g; Fiber: 4g; Protein: 4g; Sodium: 65mg

Charred Corn on the Cob

VEGETARIAN, GLUTEN-FREE *If you don't have a grill or don't want to fire it up just for corn on the cob, this is a worthy alternative. It's a healthier, pared-down take on elote, or Mexican street corn.*

PREP: 5 MINUTES • PRESSURE: 2 MINUTES • TOTAL: 25 MINUTES
PRESSURE LEVEL: HIGH • RELEASE: QUICK

SERVES 4

4 cups water

4 ears corn, shucked and halved

½ teaspoon canola oil

1 tablespoon finely grated Parmesan cheese

Kosher salt

Freshly ground black pepper

⅛ teaspoon paprika

1 tablespoon finely chopped fresh parsley

1. Add the water and corn to the Instant Pot. Secure the lid.

2. Select Manual and cook at high pressure for 2 minutes.

3. Once cooking is complete, use a quick release. Once all of the steam has escaped, open the lid and, using tongs, transfer the corn to a paper towel–lined platter or a cooling rack.

4. Carefully pour the water out and dry the pot completely.

5. Select Sauté on high heat. Once hot, add the oil. Add the corn and quickly toss with the oil.

6. Cook in one layer without moving for 4 minutes or until charred. Rotate the corn and repeat twice until a few sides are charred.

7. Using tongs, remove the corn from the pot and place on a platter. Sprinkle with half of the Parmesan and season with salt, pepper, and a sprinkle of paprika. Turn the corn and repeat to season the other side, finishing with a sprinkle of parsley.

INSTANT POT TIP: This recipe also works with the Steam function. Instead of the first two steps, add 1 cup water to the pot and put the steam rack in. Put the corn on the steam rack and secure the lid. Select Steam and cook for 3 minutes before using a quick release. Follow the rest of the recipe as written.

Per Serving Calories: 87; Total Carbohydrates: 15g; Saturated Fat: 1g; Trans Fat: 0g; Fiber: 2g; Protein: 4g; Sodium: 105mg

Corn Pudding

VEGETARIAN, GLUTEN-FREE *Like a cross between cornbread, soufflé, and pudding, this side dish will have everyone asking for more. When cutting the corn off the cob, be sure to scrape the juicy bits from the cob with the back of your knife. For an extra indulgence, top with grated cheese after it's cooked and broil for a few minutes.*

PREP: 10 MINUTES • PRESSURE: 30 MINUTES • TOTAL: 45 MINUTES
PRESSURE LEVEL: LOW • RELEASE: QUICK

SERVES 4

2 tablespoons butter

2 shallots, finely chopped

1 cup fresh corn, cut off the cob

¾ cup whole milk

¼ cup sour cream

3 tablespoons cornmeal

1 tablespoon sugar

2 eggs, beaten

½ teaspoon kosher salt

¼ teaspoon freshly ground black pepper

1½ cups water

1. Preheat the Instant Pot by selecting Sauté.

2. Once hot, add the butter. Once the butter has melted, add the shallots and select Cancel. Sauté until the sizzling stops.

3. In a medium bowl, combine the corn, milk, sour cream, cornmeal, sugar, eggs, salt, and pepper. Add the butter and shallots and stir until well combined.

4. Add the water to the Instant Pot and place the steam rack on top. Butter a 6- or 7-inch round baking dish, pour the mixture into it, and cover with foil. Carefully lower the pan onto the rack and secure the lid.

5. Select Manual and cook at low pressure for 30 minutes.

6. Once cooking is complete, use a quick release. Very carefully remove the pan. Let it cool a few minutes before serving.

COOKING TIP: If you have two baking dishes that stack nicely on top of each other, you can double the recipe. This does not affect the cooking time.

Per Serving Calories: 207; Total Carbohydrates: 19g; Saturated Fat: 7g; Trans Fat: 0g; Fiber: 1g; Protein: 6g; Sodium: 391mg

Sesame Bok Choy

VEGETARIAN *Bok choy is a Chinese cabbage that's full of valuable nutrients and delicate in taste. It's easy to cook in the Instant Pot, which seals in nutrition, and can also be used in stir-fries, soups, and more. Here, bok choy is steamed and tossed with sesame oil and soy sauce for a simple side dish.*

PREP: 5 MINUTES • PRESSURE: 4 MINUTES • TOTAL: 20 MINUTES
PRESSURE LEVEL: HIGH • RELEASE: QUICK

SERVES 4

1 cup water

1 medium head bok choy (see Ingredient Tip), leaves separated

1 teaspoon soy sauce

½ teaspoon sesame oil

2 teaspoons sesame seeds

Kosher salt

Freshly ground black pepper

1. Add the water to the Instant Pot and place the steamer basket or rack on top. Stack the bok choy on top, with the largest/thickest leaves on the bottom. Secure the lid.

2. Select Manual and cook at high pressure for 4 minutes.

3. Once cooking is complete, use a quick release.

4. Carefully transfer the bok choy to a large bowl and toss with the soy sauce, sesame oil, and sesame seeds. Season with salt and pepper as desired.

INGREDIENT TIP: Bok choy is not to be confused with baby bok choy, which is too small to cook in the pressure cooker without turning to mush. It's the size of a large head of romaine lettuce. If you can't find it at your market, use Napa cabbage instead.

Per Serving Calories: 54; Total Carbohydrates: 5g; Saturated Fat: 0g; Trans Fat: 0g; Fiber: 2g; Protein: 3g; Sodium: 249mg

Braised Cabbage

GLUTEN-FREE *Cabbage is an easy side dish that's often overlooked for flashier vegetables, but can add real flavor and nutrition to your meal. In this recipe, fresh cabbage cooks with salty bacon for just 3 minutes. Serve as an accompaniment to sausages, corned beef, or pot roast.*

PREP: 5 MINUTES • PRESSURE: 3 MINUTES • TOTAL: 15 MINUTES
PRESSURE LEVEL: HIGH • RELEASE: QUICK

SERVES 6 TO 8

3 bacon slices

1 tablespoon butter

1 small head green cabbage, cored, quartered, and cut into ½-inch strips

1 cup vegetable or chicken broth

Kosher salt

Freshly ground pepper

1. To preheat the Instant Pot, select Sauté.

2. Once hot, add the bacon in one layer. Cook until crisp, flipping halfway through, about 5 minutes. Carefully remove the bacon and cut into pieces.

3. Add the butter. Once the butter is melted, add the cabbage, broth, and bacon. Season with salt and pepper and stir. Secure the lid.

4. Select Manual and cook at high pressure for 3 minutes.

5. Once cooking is complete, use a quick release. Serve.

VARIATION TIP: If you're making Corned Beef (page 114) or German Sausages with Peppers and Onions (page 125), you can use the cooking liquid from the meat for extra-flavorful cabbage. Simply add the cabbage to the liquid and season with salt and pepper. Proceed with the recipe as written.

Per Serving Calories: 70; Total Carbohydrates: 7g; Saturated Fat: 2g; Trans Fat: 0g; Fiber: 3g; Protein: 4g; Sodium: 263mg

Sweet and Spicy Carrots

VEGETARIAN, GLUTEN-FREE *Carrots cook in a flash using the Steam function, and a quick Sauté with honey and a touch of spice makes them way better than plain steamed carrots. Quick-cooking the carrots also ensures that they retain all their nutrients.*

PREP: 5 MINUTES • PRESSURE: 2 MINUTES • TOTAL: 15 MINUTES
PRESSURE LEVEL: HIGH • RELEASE: QUICK

SERVES 4

1 cup water

5 to 6 large carrots, peeled and cut into 1-inch chunks (about 3 cups)

1 tablespoon butter

¼ teaspoon ground cumin

¼ teaspoon cayenne

Kosher salt

Freshly ground black pepper

2 teaspoons honey

1. Prepare the Instant Pot by adding the water to the pot and placing a steamer basket on top. Place the carrots in the steamer basket and secure the lid.

2. Select Steam and cook at high pressure for 2 minutes.

3. Once cooking is complete, use a quick release. Carefully remove the steamer basket, using oven mitts or tongs. Carefully pour the water out of the pot and completely dry the pot before replacing it.

4. Add the butter and select Sauté.

5. Once the butter has melted, add the carrots back to the pot. Stir until well coated. Add the cumin and cayenne, and season with salt and pepper. Stir.

6. Add the honey and select Cancel. Stir well until fully coated, and serve.

SUBSTITUTION TIP: Make this recipe vegan by using 1½ teaspoons agave instead of honey, and a butter substitute.

Per Serving Calories: 74; Total Carbohydrates: 12g; Saturated Fat: 2g; Trans Fat: 0g; Fiber: 2g; Protein: 1g; Sodium: 122mg

Beets with Goat Cheese

VEGETARIAN, GLUTEN-FREE   *Beets are super nutritious, look beautiful on a dinner table, and are extra easy when cooked in the pressure cooker. Serve them simply with tangy and creamy goat cheese, fresh lemon, and olive oil. Turn this into a salad by adding baby spinach and a sprinkle of toasted walnuts.*

PREP: 5 MINUTES • PRESSURE: 20 MINUTES • TOTAL: 30 MINUTES
PRESSURE LEVEL: HIGH • RELEASE: QUICK

SERVES 4

1 cup water
4 medium beets
½ cup crumbled goat cheese
Juice of ½ lemon
Extra-virgin olive oil
Kosher salt
Freshly ground black pepper

1. Prepare the Instant Pot by adding the water to the pot and placing the steamer basket on top.

2. Clean and trim the beets in the sink. Add them to the steamer basket and secure the lid.

3. Select Manual and cook at high pressure for 20 minutes.

4. Once cooking is complete, use a quick release. Pierce a beet with a knife to check for doneness. If not tender enough, return to the pot and cook for 5 minutes more.

5. If done, carefully remove the steamer basket and run the beets under cold water in the sink. Slide the skins off and slice the beets on a cutting board.

6. Arrange the sliced beets on a plate and top with the goat cheese, lemon juice, and a drizzle of olive oil, and season with salt and pepper.

INGREDIENT TIP: Beets have beautiful juice that will unfortunately stain your counters, hands, and anything else they come into contact with. Washing and peeling the beets in the sink will help, as will using a cutting board. Wear gloves if you don't want pink hands.

Per Serving Calories: 112; Total Carbohydrates: 10g; Saturated Fat: 4g; Trans Fat: 0g; Fiber: 2g; Protein: 6g; Sodium: 164mg

Spaghetti Squash with Parmesan and Pine Nuts

VEGETARIAN, GLUTEN-FREE *Spaghetti squash is a magical vegetable that, when cooked, produces spaghetti-like strands that are gluten-free and low in carbohydrates. It steams quickly in the Instant Pot, and a topping of Parmesan, pine nuts, and basil simulates the flavors of pesto without all the work. Add some crispy pancetta for a little extra oomph.*

PREP: 10 MINUTES · PRESSURE: 7 MINUTES · TOTAL: 20 MINUTES
PRESSURE LEVEL: HIGH · RELEASE: QUICK

SERVES 2 TO 4

1 (2- to 4-pound) spaghetti squash, halved crosswise

1 cup water

⅓ cup pine nuts

2 tablespoons extra-virgin olive oil

3 garlic cloves, minced

Juice of ½ lemon

⅓ cup grated Parmesan cheese

Kosher salt

Freshly ground black pepper

2 tablespoons chopped fresh basil leaves

1. Lay each squash half on its side. Scoop out all of the seeds and the stringy, fibrous innards with a spoon, leaving the two halves hollow.

2. Add the water to the Instant Pot. Set the squash inside, cut-side up. Secure the lid.

3. Select Manual and cook at high pressure for 7 minutes.

4. Meanwhile, preheat a frying or sauté pan over medium-high heat on the stove top. Add the pine nuts and toss every 30 seconds for about 3 minutes, until toasted. Set aside.

5. Add the oil to the sauté pan, followed by the garlic. Sauté for 1 minute until cooked, but not brown. Remove from the heat.

6. Once pressure cooking is complete, use a quick release. Carefully remove the squash and drain any collected water.

7. Use a fork to separate the strands from the peel, keeping the strands as long as possible. Place the strands in a large bowl. Toss with the garlic and oil, lemon juice, and most of the Parmesan. Season with salt and pepper. Top with the toasted pine nuts, more Parmesan, and basil and serve immediately.

INGREDIENT TIP: Cutting the squash crosswise ensures longer strands of "spaghetti." You can stack the halves if they won't fit in the pot side by side.

Per Serving Calories: 487; Total Carbohydrates: 37g; Saturated Fat: 6g; Trans Fat: 0g; Fiber: 1g; Protein: 11g; Sodium: 288mg

Root Vegetable Medley

VEGETARIAN, GLUTEN-FREE *This quick winter side dish showcases root vegetables at their finest. A little butter is always a great addition, and the pinch of baking soda helps the veggies brown without needing the oven. Serve with a roast chicken or pork loin and a green vegetable.*

PREP: 10 MINUTES • PRESSURE: 6 MINUTES • TOTAL: 20 MINUTES
PRESSURE LEVEL: HIGH • RELEASE: QUICK

SERVES 4 TO 6

2 tablespoons butter

1½ cups peeled butternut squash, cut into 1-inch cubes

1 cup peeled parsnips, cut into 1-inch cubes

1 cup peeled turnips, cut into 1-inch cubes

¾ cup vegetable or chicken broth

⅛ teaspoon sugar

¼ teaspoon baking soda

Kosher salt

Freshly ground black pepper

1 teaspoon finely chopped fresh rosemary

1. Preheat the Instant Pot by selecting Sauté.

2. Once hot, add the butter. Once the butter has melted, add the butternut squash and toss. Cook for 4 minutes, stirring occasionally.

3. Add the parsnips, turnips, broth, sugar, and baking soda, and season with salt and pepper. Stir and secure the lid.

4. Select Manual and cook at high pressure for 6 minutes.

5. Once cooking is complete, use a quick release. Drain off most of the liquid. Toss with the rosemary and season as needed.

VARIATION TIP: You can make this into a tasty purée. Add 1 minute to the cook time and reserve the drained liquid. Purée and add back the liquid as needed for a smooth texture.

Per Serving Calories: 117; Total Carbohydrates: 15g; Saturated Fat: 4g; Trans Fat: 0g; Fiber: 3g; Protein: 2g; Sodium: 329mg

Brown Butter Fingerling Potatoes

VEGETARIAN, GLUTEN-FREE *Don't heat up your whole oven just for roasting a small pan of potatoes. You can get even better results in the pressure cooker. Browning them with butter first builds flavor and crisps the skin, and steaming them with a small dose of broth leaves them fluffy. If you don't have rosemary, substitute parsley, tarragon, thyme, or basil.*

PREP: 5 MINUTES • PRESSURE: 7 MINUTES • TOTAL: 35 MINUTES
PRESSURE LEVEL: HIGH • RELEASE: NATURAL

SERVES 4

2 tablespoons butter

1½ pounds small fingerling potatoes, each pricked twice with a small knife

½ cup vegetable or chicken broth

Kosher salt

Freshly ground black pepper

1 fresh rosemary sprig (leaves only), minced

1. Preheat the Instant Pot by selecting Sauté on high heat.

2. Once hot, add the butter. Once the butter is mostly melted, add the potatoes. Stir to coat the potatoes.

3. Cook, stirring occasionally, for about 10 minutes, or until the skins start to get crispy and the butter is browned, but not burned.

4. Add the broth and secure the lid.

5. Select Manual and cook at high pressure for 7 minutes.

6. Once cooking is complete, use a natural release for 10 minutes, then release any remaining pressure.

7. Season with salt and pepper and top with rosemary.

COOKING TIP: The cook time in the recipe is for medium-size fingerlings, no more than 1 inch thick.

Per Serving Calories: 175; Total Carbohydrates: 27g; Saturated Fat: 4g; Trans Fat: 0g; Fiber: 3g; Protein: 4g; Sodium: 185mg

Horseradish Mashed Potatoes

VEGETARIAN, GLUTEN-FREE *A quick trip in the pressure cooker yields tender potatoes ready for mashing, making this favorite side dish extra easy. A healthy dose of sour cream and horseradish punches things up while keeping it creamy. Serve with a hearty piece of meat, like the Corned Beef on page 114.*

**PREP: 10 MINUTES • PRESSURE: 10 MINUTES • TOTAL: 30 MINUTES
PRESSURE LEVEL: HIGH • RELEASE: QUICK**

SERVES 8

4 pounds Yukon Gold potatoes, peeled and quartered

3 cups water

1 teaspoon kosher salt, plus more for seasoning

5 tablespoons butter

½ cup whole milk

1 cup sour cream

¼ cup drained prepared horseradish

Freshly ground black pepper

1. Add the potatoes, water, and salt to the Instant Pot. Secure the lid.

2. Select Manual and cook at high pressure for 10 minutes.

3. Meanwhile, in a small saucepan over low heat on the stove, heat the butter and milk just until very warm.

4. Once pressure cooking is complete, use a quick release. Test the potatoes to make sure they are tender. Carefully drain off the cooking liquid, reserving ½ cup.

5. Use a potato masher to mash the potatoes until fluffy and all lumps are gone. Add the warm milk and butter, sour cream, and horseradish. Season with pepper and gently mix until well combined.

6. If the potatoes are too thick, add cooking liquid, 1 tablespoon at a time. Taste for seasoning.

INGREDIENT TIP: Bottled prepared horseradish can typically be found in the refrigerated aisle of your grocery store. Add more if you like things spicy.

Per Serving Calories: 307; Total Carbohydrates: 43g; Saturated Fat: 9g; Trans Fat: 0g; Fiber: 3g; Protein: 6g; Sodium: 409mg

Sweet Potatoes with Brown Sugar Topping

VEGETARIAN *A quicker, healthier take on the traditional Thanksgiving side dish, whole sweet potatoes are steamed until tender, split in two, and topped with a brown sugar and butter topping. The topping gets a little crispy under the broiler, thanks to a bit of flour, making it reminiscent of a praline.*

PREP: 5 MINUTES • PRESSURE: 12–18 MINUTES • TOTAL: 40 MINUTES
PRESSURE LEVEL: HIGH • RELEASE: NATURAL

SERVES 6 TO 8

1 cup water

6 medium sweet potatoes, pricked a few times with a fork

4 tablespoons butter, cubed

½ cup brown sugar

¼ cup all-purpose flour

½ teaspoon ground cinnamon

Pinch kosher salt

1. Add the water to the Instant Pot and place the steamer basket or steam rack on top. Place the sweet potatoes in the steamer basket. Secure the lid.

2. Select Manual and cook at high pressure for 12 to 18 minutes (12 for especially small sweet potatoes, 15 for medium, and 18 for large).

3. Meanwhile, in a small bowl, mix together the butter, brown sugar, flour, cinnamon, and salt with your fingers until a well-combined but crumbly mixture is formed.

4. Once cooking is complete, use a natural release for 10 minutes, then release any remaining pressure.

5. Preheat the oven to broil.

6. Carefully transfer the potatoes to a baking sheet. Slice each in half lengthwise and lay side by side, cut-side up. Sprinkle each half with 1 heaping tablespoon of the sugar mixture and broil for 3 to 5 minutes, until lightly crispy.

VARIATION TIP: This technique would also work with marshmallows in place of the brown sugar topping. Place the sweet potato halves close together so that they are touching on the baking sheet and top with mini marshmallows before broiling.

Per Serving Calories: 310; Total Carbohydrates: 58g; Saturated Fat: 5g; Trans Fat: 0g; Fiber: 6g; Protein: 3g; Sodium: 98mg

Chipotle Black Beans

VEGETARIAN, GLUTEN-FREE *Dried beans, when properly cooked, have better flavor and texture than their canned counterparts. The pressure cooker makes preparing dried beans foolproof while saving you time and money. This recipe has a rich smokiness thanks to a dose of chili powder and chipotles in adobo.*

PREP: 5 MINUTES · PRESSURE: 15 MINUTES · TOTAL: 35 MINUTES
PRESSURE LEVEL: HIGH · RELEASE: NATURAL

SERVES 6 TO 8

2 tablespoons canola oil

1 medium onion, finely diced

1 small bell pepper, finely diced

4 garlic cloves, minced

1 tablespoon chili powder

2 teaspoons ground cumin

1 small can chipotles in adobo, roughly chopped

1 pound dried black beans, rinsed, picked over (discard any bad beans), and soaked overnight

8 cups vegetable or chicken broth or water

2 teaspoons kosher salt

1. Preheat the Instant Pot by selecting Sauté. Add the oil to the pot.

2. Once hot, add the onion, bell pepper, and garlic. Stir and cook for 2 minutes, until the onion starts to become translucent.

3. Add the chili powder and cumin and stir, cooking for 1 minute. Add the chipotles and stir.

4. Add the beans, broth, and salt and stir. Secure the lid.

5. Select Manual and cook at high pressure for 15 minutes.

6. Once cooking is complete, select Cancel and use a natural release.

7. Taste the beans for doneness and seasoning. If the beans aren't as soft as you'd like, return to high pressure for 1 to 3 minutes and use a natural release.

INGREDIENT TIP: Chipotles in adobo come in a can or jar and can be found in the international food section of the grocery store.

Per Serving Calories: 375; Total Carbohydrates: 54g; Saturated Fat: 1g; Trans Fat: 0g; Fiber: 13g; Protein: 24g; Sodium: 1885mg

Homemade Hummus

GLUTEN-FREE, VEGETARIAN *This homemade hummus is made with dried chickpeas, which are cooked in no time in the pressure cooker—no soaking required. Don't forget the first dose of oil, since it helps keep the beans from foaming too much in the pot. Start by making the recipe as written and then adjust it according to your taste, adding spices, herbs, and more.*

PREP: 10 MINUTES • PRESSURE: 45 MINUTES
TOTAL: 1 HOUR, 10 MINUTES • PRESSURE LEVEL: HIGH
RELEASE: NATURAL

SERVES 8 TO 10

- 8 ounces dried chickpeas, rinsed and picked over (discard any bad beans)
- 4 cups water
- 6 tablespoons extra-virgin olive oil, divided
- ⅓ cup tahini
- ¼ cup freshly squeezed lemon juice
- 3 garlic cloves, minced
- 1½ teaspoons kosher salt
- ½ teaspoon smoked paprika (optional)

1. Add the chickpeas, water, and 2 tablespoons of oil to the Instant Pot and secure the lid.

2. Select Manual and cook at high pressure for 45 minutes.

3. Once cooking is complete, use a natural release. This will take about 15 minutes.

4. Test the chickpeas for doneness—they should be soft but not mushy. If they're not soft enough, cook for 3 to 5 minutes more on high pressure.

5. Carefully drain the chickpeas and reserve 1 cup of cooking liquid. Purée the chickpeas in a food processor with the remaining 4 tablespoons of oil, tahini, lemon juice, garlic, salt, paprika (if using), and ¼ cup of reserved cooking liquid. Add more liquid as needed to reach the desired consistency.

6. Serve or store for up to 5 days in the refrigerator.

INGREDIENT TIP: Chickpeas are also known as garbanzo beans. Tahini is a sesame seed paste that's typically found in a jar and keeps for months in the refrigerator.

Per Serving Calories: 264; Total Carbohydrates: 20g; Saturated Fat: 3g; Trans Fat: 0g; Fiber: 6g; Protein: 8g; Sodium: 459mg

Chickpea Curry

VEGETARIAN, GLUTEN-FREE *For a simple vegan curry, chickpeas provide a hearty base. Fresh veggies make this dish extra healthy, and garlic and curry powder lend the curry a spiced but not spicy flavor. Serve over steamy jasmine rice or with warm naan.*

PREP: 10 MINUTES • PRESSURE: 5 MINUTES • TOTAL: 30 MINUTES
PRESSURE LEVEL: HIGH • RELEASE: NATURAL

SERVES 4 TO 6

2 tablespoons extra-virgin olive oil

1 onion, diced

1 small green bell pepper, diced

2 large garlic cloves, minced

1 tablespoon curry powder

2 (15-ounce) cans chickpeas, rinsed and drained

1 (14.5-ounce) can crushed or diced tomatoes with juice

1 cup frozen corn

1 cup frozen sliced okra

1 packed cup chopped kale leaves

1 cup vegetable or chicken broth

1 tablespoon sugar or honey

1 teaspoon kosher salt

¼ teaspoon freshly ground black pepper

Juice of 1 lime

2 tablespoons cilantro leaves

1. Preheat the Instant Pot by selecting Sauté.

2. Once hot, add the oil and onion and stir. Cook for 4 minutes until the onion is translucent and starting to brown. Add the bell pepper and garlic and cook for 2 minutes more.

3. Add the curry powder and stir. Cook for 30 seconds before adding the chickpeas, tomatoes with juice, corn, okra, kale, broth, and sugar or honey. Stir and secure the lid.

4. Select Manual and cook at high pressure for 5 minutes.

5. Once cooking is complete, use a natural release.

6. Add the salt, pepper, and lime juice. Stir and taste, adding more salt as needed.

7. Top with cilantro leaves and serve.

SUBSTITUTION TIP: If you don't like cilantro, use flat-leaf parsley instead.

Per Serving Calories: 430; Total Carbohydrates: 58g; Saturated Fat: 2g; Trans Fat: 0g; Fiber: 13g; Protein: 20g; Sodium: 811mg

No-Fry Refried Beans

VEGETARIAN, GLUTEN-FREE *These beans may not technically be refried, but they have the same great flavor and texture as the classic south-of-the-border dish, without all of the time, effort, or fat. Oil helps prevent foaming, and a quick mash yields a creamy side dish. A sprinkle of cheese and a squeeze of lime wouldn't hurt.*

PREP: 10 MINUTES • PRESSURE: 35 MINUTES • TOTAL: 1 HOUR
PRESSURE LEVEL: HIGH • RELEASE: NATURAL

MAKES 5 CUPS
(8 TO 10 SERVINGS)

1 pound dried pinto beans, rinsed and picked over (discard any bad beans)

3 tablespoons canola oil

2 garlic cloves, minced

1 medium onion, diced

3 cilantro sprigs, with stems, chopped

8 cups water

1½ teaspoons kosher salt

1. Add the beans, oil, garlic, onion, cilantro, and water to the pot. Secure the lid.

2. Select Manual and cook at high pressure for 35 minutes.

3. When cooking is complete, select Cancel and use a natural release. This will take about 15 minutes.

4. Carefully drain the beans, reserving 2 cups of cooking liquid.

5. Return the beans to the pot and add back 1 cup of cooking liquid. Add the salt.

6. Mash the beans well with a potato masher or use an immersion blender. If the mixture is dry, add more cooking liquid ¼ cup at a time until the desired texture is reached. Taste and season again if needed.

7. Store leftovers in individual containers and freeze for up to 3 months.

COOKING TIP: There's no need to soak your beans for this recipe—they'll turn out nice and tender and it only adds a few minutes of cook time.

Per Serving Calories: 250; Total Carbohydrates: 37g; Saturated Fat: 1g; Trans Fat: 0g; Fiber: 9g; Protein: 12g; Sodium: 446mg

Southern-Style Black-Eyed Peas

GLUTEN-FREE *Black-eyed peas—a type of bean—are a staple of the South, and are almost always cooked with some form of pork. Here, bacon lends a salty and smoky note that pairs nicely with the earthy beans. Eat them on New Year's Day to ensure good luck for the year.*

PREP: 10 MINUTES • PRESSURE: 10 MINUTES • TOTAL: 30 MINUTES
PRESSURE LEVEL: HIGH • RELEASE: NATURAL

SERVES 4 TO 5

3 thick-cut bacon slices

1 tablespoon canola oil

1 small onion, diced

2 garlic cloves, minced

8 ounces black-eyed peas, rinsed, picked over (discard any bad beans), and soaked for at least 6 hours

4 cups chicken broth or water

1 bay leaf

Kosher salt

Freshly ground black pepper

1. To preheat your Instant Pot, select Sauté.

2. When hot, add the bacon. Cook until lightly crispy and turn to cook the other side. Remove the bacon, cut into a few pieces, and set aside.

3. Add the oil, onion, and garlic. Stir and cook for 3 minutes until the onion is translucent.

4. Add the bacon, black-eyed peas, broth or water, and bay leaf and stir. Secure the lid.

5. Select Manual and cook at high pressure for 10 minutes.

6. Once cooking is complete, use a natural release.

7. Carefully drain the beans, remove the bay leaf, and season with salt and pepper. If the beans aren't quite cooked, return to high pressure for 3 minutes.

COOKING TIP: If you didn't plan ahead and soak your beans, don't worry! Simply add 10 minutes to the cook time.

Per Serving Calories: 196; Total Carbohydrates: 11g; Saturated Fat: 3g; Trans Fat: 0g; Fiber: 2g; Protein: 13g; Sodium: 1077mg

Lentils with Tomato and Pancetta

GLUTEN-FREE *Lentils typically benefit from a couple of aromatics and a slow simmer, but pressure cooking intensifies the flavor and cuts the time in half. Pancetta adds salt, meat, and fat, and tomatoes make a rich sauce. Serve the lentils over polenta or rice, or as a side dish.*

PREP: 10 MINUTES • PRESSURE: 15 MINUTES • TOTAL: 35 MINUTES
PRESSURE LEVEL: HIGH • RELEASE: NATURAL

SERVES 5 TO 6

1 tablespoon extra-virgin olive oil

6 ounces pancetta, cut into ¼-inch cubes

1 small red onion, chopped

1 carrot, diced

2 small celery stalks, chopped

½ teaspoon kosher salt, plus more for seasoning

¼ teaspoon freshly ground black pepper

2 medium tomatoes, diced

1½ cups dried green lentils

2 cups chicken broth or water

1. To preheat the Instant Pot, select Sauté.

2. Once hot, add the oil. Add the pancetta and stir. Add the onion and stir again, cooking for 30 seconds.

3. Add the carrot and celery. Stir and cook for 2 minutes, or until the onion starts to become translucent. Add the salt and pepper.

4. Add the tomatoes, lentils, and broth or water and stir. Secure the lid.

5. Select Manual and cook at high pressure for 15 minutes.

6. Once cooking is complete, use a natural release. Taste the lentils for doneness and seasoning.

7. If they are not soft enough, cook on the Sauté setting for 5 to 10 minutes. This will also reduce any excess liquid.

VARIATION TIP: To turn this into a soup, add 1 to 2 more cups of broth.

Per Serving Calories: 448; Total Carbohydrates: 40g; Saturated Fat: 5g; Trans Fat: 0g; Fiber: 19g; Protein: 30g; Sodium: 1344mg

Creamy White Bean Dip

VEGETARIAN, GLUTEN-FREE *For a healthy snack that feels indulgent, try this creamy dip made with white beans. Cooking the dried beans in the pressure cooker means better flavor and texture without a long wait time. Serve with pita chips and carrot sticks for dipping.*

PREP: 5 MINUTES • PRESSURE: 30 MINUTES • TOTAL: 55 MINUTES
PRESSURE LEVEL: HIGH • RELEASE: NATURAL

MAKES ABOUT 3 CUPS

8 ounces dried white beans (Great Northern), rinsed and picked over (discard any bad beans)

4 cups water

3 garlic cloves, minced

2 teaspoons extra-virgin olive oil, plus more for garnish

½ teaspoon kosher salt

¼ teaspoon freshly ground black pepper

Juice of ½ lemon, plus additional if desired

½ teaspoon finely chopped fresh rosemary leaves

1. Add the beans, water, garlic, oil, salt, and pepper to the Instant Pot. Secure the lid.

2. Select Manual and cook at high pressure for 30 minutes.

3. Select Cancel and use a natural release. This will take about 15 minutes.

4. Carefully drain the beans and reserve 1 cup of cooking liquid. Purée the beans in a food processor or mash well in a large bowl until creamy. If the purée is too thick, add cooking liquid, 1 tablespoon at a time.

5. Add the lemon juice and rosemary, and season with salt and pepper. Mix well and add more lemon juice or seasoning if desired.

6. Drizzle with oil and serve.

INGREDIENT TIP: For an even faster cook time, soak the beans overnight and cut the pressure-cooking time by half.

Per Serving (⅓ cup) Calories: 95; Total Carbohydrates: 16g; Saturated Fat: 0g; Trans Fat: 0g; Fiber: 4g; Protein: 6g; Sodium: 132mg

Super-Fast Red Beans and Rice

GLUTEN-FREE *Make beans and rice extra fast by cooking them together in the pressure cooker. Long-grain white rice and canned red beans happily simmer together in the pressure cooker along with salty bacon. It's a simple but satisfying dish that uses pantry staples, so it's a great recipe to have in your back pocket.*

PREP: 10 MINUTES • PRESSURE: 5 MINUTES • TOTAL: 30 MINUTES
PRESSURE LEVEL: HIGH • RELEASE: NATURAL

SERVES 4

3 bacon slices, chopped into ¼-inch pieces

1 onion, chopped

1 bell pepper, chopped

4 garlic cloves, minced

2 large pinches cayenne

1 cup long-grain white rice

2 (15-ounce) cans red kidney beans, rinsed and drained

2 cups chicken broth

Kosher salt

Freshly ground black pepper

1. To preheat the Instant Pot, select Sauté.

2. Once hot, add the bacon and cook until lightly crisp. Remove and set aside.

3. Add the onion and sauté for 2 minutes. Add the bell pepper and cook for 2 minutes more. Add the garlic and cook for 1 minute more, until the onion is translucent.

4. Add the cayenne and bacon and stir. Add the rice, beans, and broth and stir. Season with salt and pepper. Secure the lid.

5. Select Manual and cook at high pressure for 5 minutes.

6. Once the cooking is complete, use a natural release for 10 minutes, then release any remaining pressure.

DID YOU KNOW? Beans and rice come together to form a complete protein, making the combination more than just delicious.

Per Serving Calories: 431; Total Carbohydrates: 74g; Saturated Fat: 1g; Trans Fat: 0g; Fiber: 12g; Protein: 21g; Sodium: 1218mg

Mexican-Style Brown Rice

VEGETARIAN, GLUTEN-FREE *This Tex-Mex side dish is an upgraded version of the rice that's typically served at American Mexican restaurants, and uses healthy brown rice instead of white. The rice is toasted in oil first to give it a nice texture, then cooked with tomato sauce and aromatics. Serve with black beans like the ones on page 52, or refried beans like the ones on page 55, and enchiladas or tacos.*

**PREP: 10 MINUTES • PRESSURE: 23 MINUTES • TOTAL: 45 MINUTES
PRESSURE LEVEL: HIGH • RELEASE: NATURAL**

SERVES 5 TO 6

3 tablespoons canola oil

1½ cups brown rice

1 small onion, diced

2 garlic cloves, minced

¼ teaspoon ground cumin

1 (8-ounce) can plain tomato sauce

1⅓ cups water or chicken broth

¼ teaspoon kosher salt, plus more if needed

2 tablespoons finely chopped cilantro leaves

1. Preheat the Instant Pot by selecting Sauté. Add the oil.

2. Add the rice and onion and cook, stirring, for 3 minutes. Add the garlic and cumin and cook for 1 minute more.

3. Add the tomato sauce, water or broth, and salt. Stir. Secure the lid.

4. Select Manual and cook at high pressure for 23 minutes.

5. Once cooking is complete, use a natural release for 10 minutes, then release any remaining pressure.

6. Add the cilantro and more salt if needed. Serve.

INSTANT POT TIP: The Rice function is not recommended for varieties of rice other than white rice, so it's not the best setting for this recipe.

Per Serving Calories: 314; Total Carbohydrates: 48g; Saturated Fat: 1g; Trans Fat: 0g; Fiber: 3g; Protein: 6g; Sodium: 635mg

Brown Butter and Asparagus Risotto

VEGETARIAN, GLUTEN-FREE *Don't spend your evening standing over a pot of risotto and stirring, stirring, stirring. Instead, let the pressure cooker do the hard work for you. This version combines fresh roasted asparagus with brown butter, shallots, and Parmesan cheese. It's a creamy side dish for meat or a meal all on its own.*

PREP: 15 MINUTES • PRESSURE: 6 MINUTES • TOTAL: 30 MINUTES
PRESSURE LEVEL: HIGH • RELEASE: QUICK

SERVES 5 TO 6

1 pound asparagus, cut into 1-inch pieces

1 tablespoon extra-virgin olive oil

Kosher salt

Freshly ground black pepper

5 tablespoons butter

4 medium shallots, chopped

4 garlic cloves, minced

½ cup dry white wine

4 cups good-quality vegetable or chicken broth, preferably homemade (try the recipes on pages 141 and 140)

2 cups Arborio or Calrose rice

¼ cup or more heavy cream (optional)

½ cup finely grated Parmesan cheese, plus more for serving

1. Preheat the oven to 400°F.

2. Toss the asparagus pieces in the oil and arrange in a single layer on a baking sheet. Season with salt and pepper. Roast for 10 to 15 minutes (depending on the size of the asparagus), until tender but still a little crisp.

3. Preheat the Instant Pot by selecting Sauté. Add the butter.

4. Cook, swirling around with a spoon, for about 3 minutes, or until the butter is a light brown color. Add the shallots and cook for 2 minutes. Add the garlic and cook for 1 minute more.

5. Add the wine. Stir and cook for about 3 minutes, or until the alcohol smell has gone away and much of the wine has evaporated.

6. Add the broth and rice and stir. Season with salt and pepper. Secure the lid.

7. Select Manual and cook at high pressure for 6 minutes. ▶

Brown Butter and Asparagus Risotto (continued)

8. Once cooking is complete, use a quick release. Stir. If the risotto is too soupy, select Sauté and cook, uncovered, for a few minutes. Add the cream (if using) and Parmesan and taste for seasoning.

9. Stir in the asparagus, reserving a few pieces to display on top. Serve topped with the reserved asparagus and a healthy dose of Parmesan.

VARIATION TIP: For pea risotto, omit the asparagus and skip the roasting step. Stir in 1 to 2 cups fresh or frozen peas just after pressure cooking.

Per Serving Calories: 441; Total Carbohydrates: 50g; Saturated Fat: 11g; Trans Fat: 0g; Fiber: 2g; Protein: 14g; Sodium: 835mg

Faster-than-Fast-Food Fried Rice

VEGETARIAN *Fried rice is typically made with leftover, cold rice, but sometimes you want fried rice and you want it now. In that case, you can cook the rice and fry it in just 30 minutes using just one pot. This makes an excellent side dish for a stir-fry.*

PREP: 10 MINUTES • PRESSURE: ABOUT 10 MINUTES
TOTAL: 35 MINUTES • PRESSURE LEVEL: LOW • RELEASE: NATURAL

SERVES 4

2 cups long-grain white rice

3 cups water

½ teaspoon kosher salt

2 tablespoons canola oil

10 scallions, finely chopped

2 eggs, lightly beaten

3 tablespoons soy sauce

1. Add the rice, water, and salt to the Instant Pot and secure the lid.

2. Select Rice and cook for the automated amount of time (8 to 15 minutes).

3. Once cooking is complete, select Cancel and let naturally release for 10 minutes. Release any remaining steam.

4. Stir the rice and push it up against the sides, exposing the bottom of the pot in the middle.

5. Select Sauté on high heat. Wait 1 minute and add the oil to the bottom of the pot.

6. Add the scallions and eggs to the oil. Use a spoon or spatula to break up and scramble the eggs and scrape the bottom of the pot.

7. Once the eggs are mostly cooked, stir them into the rice and cook, stirring, for a few minutes. Select Cancel, add the soy sauce, and stir.

INSTANT POT TIP: You can also use the Manual setting, or swap out the white rice for brown. Consult your Instant Pot manual or the Electric Pressure Cooking Time Charts at the back of this book for the correct cook times.

Per Serving Calories: 449; Total Carbohydrates: 78g; Saturated Fat: 1g; Trans Fat: 0g; Fiber: 2g; Protein: 11g; Sodium: 1009mg

Quinoa Tabbouleh

VEGETARIAN, GLUTEN-FREE *Tabbouleh is traditionally made with bulgur wheat, but this version uses high-protein, gluten-free quinoa instead. Chopped cucumber, tomato, mint, and garlic add fresh flavor to this side dish. Serve with kebabs or a Greek salad, along with pita and Homemade Hummus (page 53).*

PREP: 5 MINUTES • PRESSURE: 1 MINUTE • TOTAL: 20 MINUTES
PRESSURE LEVEL: HIGH • RELEASE: NATURAL

SERVES 4 TO 6

1 cup quinoa, rinsed and drained

1⅔ cups water

2 tablespoons extra-virgin olive oil, divided

½ teaspoon kosher salt, plus more as needed

1 medium tomato, finely chopped and seeded

1 small cucumber, finely chopped

1 large garlic clove, minced

⅓ cup finely chopped fresh mint and/or parsley

Juice of 1 lemon

Freshly ground black pepper

1. Add the quinoa, water, 1 tablespoon of oil, and the salt to the Instant Pot. Secure the lid.

2. Select Manual and cook at high pressure for 1 minute.

3. Once cooking is complete, use a natural release. Transfer the quinoa to a large bowl and let it cool for a few minutes.

4. Add the tomato, cucumber, garlic, mint and/or parsley, remaining 1 tablespoon of oil, and the lemon juice. Mix and season with salt and pepper.

VARIATION TIP: Turn this into a full-blown salad with dressed spinach, feta cheese, and toasted almonds.

Per Serving Calories: 256; Total Carbohydrates: 35g; Saturated Fat: 1g; Trans Fat: 0g; Fiber: 4g; Protein: 8g; Sodium: 297mg

Rustic Herb Stuffing

VEGETARIAN *If your holidays are anything like mine, space in your oven is at a premium. It leaves me scrambling for other ways to cook dishes so that everything is warm at the same time. That's when I figured out I could cook stuffing (also known as dressing) in the pressure cooker. I finish it off in the oven to crisp up, but you can skip this step if you don't care about a crunchy top.*

PREP: 10 MINUTES • PRESSURE: 20 MINUTES • TOTAL: 45 MINUTES
PRESSURE LEVEL: LOW • RELEASE: QUICK

SERVES 6

6 tablespoons butter

1 onion, chopped (about 1 cup)

3 large shallots, diced

1 cup chopped celery

8 cups plain dried bread cubes (see Ingredient Tip)

1 heaping tablespoon chopped fresh sage

1 tablespoon chopped fresh parsley

2 teaspoons chopped fresh rosemary leaves

1 teaspoon chopped fresh thyme

1 teaspoon kosher salt

¼ teaspoon freshly ground black pepper

2 eggs, beaten

2½ cups vegetable or chicken broth

1. Preheat the Instant Pot by selecting Sauté.

2. Add the butter. Once melted, add the onion, shallots, and celery. Sauté for 5 minutes, until translucent. Select Cancel and transfer the veggies and butter to a large bowl.

3. Add the dried bread, sage, parsley, rosemary, thyme, salt, pepper, eggs, and broth to the bowl. Mix just until well combined.

4. Add the mixture to the butter-coated pot. Press very lightly and secure the lid.

5. Select Manual and cook at low pressure for 20 minutes.

6. Preheat the oven to 375°F.

7. Once cooking is complete, use a quick release. Using a large serving spoon, scoop out the stuffing onto a large rimmed baking sheet.

8. Bake for 10 to 15 minutes or until crisp on top.

INGREDIENT TIP: You can use packaged dried bread cubes for this recipe or make your own. To make your own, cut white bread into ½-inch cubes. Spread out on a baking sheet and bake, stirring occasionally, in a 250°F oven for 45 minutes to 1 hour, or until dried out.

Per Serving Calories: 180; Total Carbohydrates: 9g; Saturated Fat: 8g; Trans Fat: 0g; Fiber: 1g; Protein: 5g; Sodium: 885mg

Whole-Wheat Creamy Mac and Cheese

VEGETARIAN *Ooey-gooey mac and cheese is made a little healthier with whole-wheat macaroni, but doesn't skimp on the cheesy goodness. Everyone will gobble up this decadent side dish. Add crispy bacon, fresh peas, or chopped tomatoes at the end if you want to mix it up.*

PREP: 10 MINUTES • PRESSURE: 4–5 MINUTES • TOTAL: 20 MINUTES
PRESSURE LEVEL: HIGH • RELEASE: QUICK

SERVES 6

1 pound uncooked whole-wheat macaroni

3 tablespoons butter

1 teaspoon yellow mustard

1 tablespoon kosher salt

¼ teaspoon freshly ground black pepper

4 cups water

1 (12-ounce) can evaporated milk

10 ounces shredded sharp Cheddar cheese

8 ounces shredded Monterey Jack cheese

2 ounces grated Parmesan cheese

1 cup plain breadcrumbs (optional)

1. Add the macaroni, butter, mustard, salt, pepper, and water to the Instant Pot. Stir and secure the lid.

2. Select Manual and cook at high pressure for half of the pasta package cooking time minus 1 minute. For example, if the cook time is 10 minutes, cook at high pressure for 4 minutes.

3. Once the cooking is complete, use a quick release. Carefully place a kitchen towel over the steam valve at first to prevent a hot spray.

4. Check the pasta for doneness. If it's not cooked enough, select Sauté and cook with the top off for 2 to 3 minutes until done.

5. Select Sauté and add the evaporated milk. Stir well. Add the Cheddar, Monterey Jack, and Parmesan one handful at a time, stirring after each.

6. Serve immediately or, if desired, transfer to a baking dish and top with breadcrumbs. Broil for a few minutes for a crispy topping.

SUBSTITUTION TIP: You can change out these cheeses based on your preference using pepper Jack, mild Cheddar, mozzarella, and more.

Per Serving Calories: 754; Total Carbohydrates: 64g; Saturated Fat: 25g; Trans Fat: 0g; Fiber: 6g; Protein: 39g; Sodium: 1863mg

Cheese Grits

VEGETARIAN, GLUTEN-FREE *Grits are a Southern specialty, and while they can be a bit bland on their own, a little butter and cheese turns them into a rich, tasty side dish. Serve them with breakfast or brunch, or top them with tender meat or spicy shrimp. I like mine topped with the Lentils with Tomato and Pancetta from page 57.*

PREP: 5 MINUTES • PRESSURE: 15 MINUTES • TOTAL: 35 MINUTES
PRESSURE LEVEL: LOW • RELEASE: NATURAL

SERVES 4

1 cup coarse-ground cornmeal (grits)

3½ cups water

1½ teaspoons kosher salt

½ teaspoon freshly ground black pepper

4 tablespoons butter, cut into pieces

1 cup shredded Cheddar cheese

1. Add the cornmeal, water, salt, pepper, and butter to the Instant Pot. Stir and secure the lid.

2. Select Manual and cook at low pressure for 15 minutes.

3. Once cooking is complete, let naturally release for 10 minutes, then release any remaining steam.

4. Immediately add the cheese and whisk vigorously until smooth and slightly cooled. Serve immediately.

VARIATION TIP: If you'd like to make this recipe a little healthier, decrease the butter to 2 tablespoons and halve the cheese. I recommend using a strong-tasting cheese in this case, like extra-sharp Cheddar.

Per Serving Calories: 326; Total Carbohydrates: 24g; Saturated Fat: 13g; Trans Fat: 0g; Fiber: 5g; Protein: 9g; Sodium: 1136mg

CHAPTER FIVE
SOUPS, STEWS, AND CHILIES

Vegan Black Bean Soup with Avocado Salsa

VEGETARIAN, GLUTEN-FREE *This richly flavored black bean soup is cooked from dried beans—no soaking required—in a little over an hour. Roasted poblanos add mild but deep flavor, and a cool topping of avocado salsa makes this more than just your average black bean soup.*

PREP: 20 MINUTES • PRESSURE: 30 MINUTES • TOTAL: 1 HOUR, 10 MINUTES • PRESSURE LEVEL: HIGH • RELEASE: NATURAL

1. Preheat the oven to broil.

2. Rub the poblanos with 1 teaspoon of oil. Broil until blistered on all sides. Once cool enough to handle, slide off any loose skin, remove the stem and seeds, and chop the poblanos.

3. Preheat the Instant Pot by selecting Sauté. Once hot, add the remaining 2 tablespoons of oil followed by all but ¼ cup of the onion, the bell pepper, and the garlic. Stir and cook for about 3 minutes, until the onion softens.

4. Add the roasted poblano, cumin, chili powder, and oregano. Stir and cook for 1 minute. Add the beans, bay leaf, and broth, and season with salt and pepper. Secure the lid.

5. Select Manual and cook at high pressure for 30 minutes.

6. Meanwhile, in a medium bowl, combine the avocados, tomato, the reserved ¼ cup of diced onion, the cilantro, and a squeeze of lime juice. Season with salt and pepper.

7. Once cooking is complete, use a natural release for about 15 minutes. Remove the bay leaf.

8. Add the remaining lime juice to the pot. The liquid will thicken upon standing. If desired, purée up to half of the soup with an immersion blender or in a countertop blender. Serve hot, topped with avocado salsa.

VARIATION TIP: If you're not eating vegan, add a dollop of sour cream.

Per Serving Calories: 527; Total Carbohydrates: 63g; Saturated Fat: 4g; Trans Fat: 0g; Fiber: 18g; Protein: 25g; Sodium: 940mg

SERVES 6 TO 8

2 poblano peppers

2 tablespoons plus 1 teaspoon extra-virgin olive oil, divided

1 large yellow onion, finely diced, ¼ cup reserved

1 bell pepper, finely diced

5 garlic cloves, minced

2 teaspoons ground cumin

2 teaspoons chili powder

1 teaspoon dried oregano

1 pound dried black beans, rinsed and picked over (discard any bad beans)

1 bay leaf

7 cups vegetable broth (try the recipe on page 141)

Kosher salt

Freshly ground black pepper

2 medium avocados, peeled, pitted, diced, and tossed with 1 tablespoon freshly squeezed lime juice

1 large tomato or 2 small tomatoes, chopped

2 tablespoons chopped cilantro

1 lime, halved

Fresh Tomato Soup

VEGETARIAN, GLUTEN-FREE *At the end of the summer, a final bumper crop of beautiful tomatoes arrives. Even if you're sick of eating fresh tomatoes all summer, the tasty beauties can be used to make a fantastic soup. Serve this forgivingly simple dish with crusty garlic bread.*

**PREP: 15 MINUTES • PRESSURE: 15 MINUTES • TOTAL: 45 MINUTES
PRESSURE LEVEL: HIGH • RELEASE: NATURAL**

1. To preheat the Instant Pot, select Sauté.

2. Once hot, add the oil followed by the onion and carrot. Cook for 6 to 7 minutes, until the onion is translucent. Add the garlic and cook for 2 minutes more.

3. Add the tomatoes, sugar, tomato paste, and broth. Season with salt and pepper. Secure the lid.

4. Select Manual and cook at high pressure for 15 minutes.

5. Once cooking is complete, let naturally release for 10 minutes. Release any remaining steam.

6. Add the cream. Use an immersion blender to purée the soup or carefully purée in batches in a blender. If there are chunks of peel and they bother you, strain the soup or run it through a food mill. Add more broth if a thinner soup is desired.

7. Taste for seasoning. Serve topped with fresh basil and Parmesan (if using).

SUBSTITUTION TIP: To make this dish Paleo, leave out the sugar and Parmesan and replace the cream with more broth.

Per Serving Calories: 239; Total Carbohydrates: 22g; Saturated Fat: 6g; Trans Fat: 0g; Fiber: 6g; Protein: 5g; Sodium: 225mg

SERVES 4

2 tablespoons extra-virgin olive oil

1 large red onion, chopped

1 large carrot, peeled and chopped

3 garlic cloves, smashed

3 pounds high-quality ripe tomatoes, coarsely chopped

1 teaspoon sugar

1 tablespoon tomato paste

¾ cup vegetable or chicken broth, plus more if needed

Kosher salt

Freshly ground black pepper

⅓ cup heavy cream

Fresh basil, for garnish (optional)

Parmesan cheese, for garnish (optional)

Creamy Cauliflower and Potato Soup

VEGETARIAN, GLUTEN-FREE *Add some much-needed nutrition to potato soup while still achieving creamy results by replacing half of the potatoes with cauliflower. Your family will never know! Notice that the cauliflower is cut into bigger pieces than the potatoes, allowing you to cook them at the same rate.*

PREP: 10 MINUTES • PRESSURE: 5 MINUTES • TOTAL: 35 MINUTES
PRESSURE LEVEL: HIGH • RELEASE: NATURAL

1. Preheat the Instant Pot by selecting Sauté.

2. Once hot, add the oil followed by the onion and garlic. Stir and cook for about 3 minutes, until the onion begins to turn translucent.

3. Add the cauliflower, potatoes, and broth. Season with salt and pepper. Secure the lid.

4. Select Manual and cook at high pressure for 5 minutes.

5. Once cooking is complete, select Cancel and let naturally release for 10 minutes. Release any remaining steam.

6. The potatoes and cauliflower should be very tender. Add the milk or half-and-half and ½ cup of cheese.

7. Blend until smooth using an immersion blender. Alternatively, blend in batches in a blender, being careful to crack the lid. Add more broth if you want a thinner soup.

8. Taste for seasoning. Serve topped with a sprinkle of the remaining Cheddar.

SUBSTITUTION TIP: Make this soup vegan by using nondairy milk and omitting the cheese.

Per Serving Calories: 354; Total Carbohydrates: 35g; Saturated Fat: 8g; Trans Fat: 0g; Fiber: 6g; Protein: 19g; Sodium: 1058mg

SERVES 4 TO 5

1 tablespoon extra-virgin olive oil

1 medium yellow onion, diced

3 garlic cloves, smashed

1 medium cauliflower head, broken into large florets

1 pound Yukon Gold potatoes, peeled and cut into ½-inch cubes

4 cups vegetable or chicken broth, plus more if needed

Kosher salt

Freshly ground black pepper

1 cup whole milk or half-and-half

1 cup shredded sharp Cheddar cheese, divided

Thai-Style Corn Chowder

VEGETARIAN *Fresh, in-season corn is totally delicious, and this 20-minute soup puts it front and center. Perfect for late summer when corn on the cob abounds, this chowder is creamy, lightly spicy, and vegan to boot.*

PREP: 10 MINUTES • PRESSURE: 3 MINUTES • TOTAL: 20 MINUTES
PRESSURE LEVEL: HIGH • RELEASE: QUICK

SERVES 4

6 ears corn, shucked

1 tablespoon extra-virgin olive oil

1 medium onion, finely diced

1 red bell pepper, finely diced

4 garlic cloves, minced

2 teaspoons sesame oil

¼ teaspoon smoked paprika

⅛ teaspoon red pepper flakes

1½ cups vegetable broth, plus extra if needed

1 (13.5-ounce) can light coconut milk

1 tablespoon soy sauce

Juice of 1 small lime

Kosher salt

Freshly ground pepper

1 heaping tablespoon chopped fresh parsley leaves, for garnish

1. On a large plate or platter, cut the corn off the cob. Use the back of your knife to scrape the juicy corn pulp off the cobs.

2. Preheat the Instant Pot by selecting Sauté.

3. Once hot, add the oil followed by the onion and bell pepper. Cook, stirring, for about 3 minutes, until the onion begins to turn translucent. Add the garlic, sesame oil, paprika, and red pepper flakes and cook for 2 minutes more.

4. Add the broth and corn along with any pulp and stir. Secure the lid.

5. Select Manual and cook at high pressure for 3 minutes.

6. Once cooking is complete, select Cancel and use a quick release.

7. Add the coconut milk, soy sauce, and lime juice. Season with salt and pepper.

8. Use an immersion blender to blend about two-thirds of the soup. Alternatively, blend two-thirds of the soup in batches in a countertop blender.

9. Recombine the smooth and chunky parts of the soup and reheat if needed. Serve sprinkled with parsley.

INGREDIENT TIP: Choose corn that's still in its leaves with light yellow silk. The kernels should be nice and plump. If possible, use the corn within a day or two of buying—it's best when super fresh.

Per Serving Calories: 400; Total Carbohydrates: 33g; Saturated Fat: 21g; Trans Fat: 0g; Fiber: 6g; Protein: 8g; Sodium: 569mg

Creamy Broccoli and Leek Soup

VEGETARIAN *Try this creamy broccoli soup for a quick and nutritious weeknight meal. It goes great with a grilled cheese sandwich, and might even get your kids to eat broccoli. Frozen broccoli will work in a pinch.*

PREP: 15 MINUTES • PRESSURE: 6 MINUTES • TOTAL: 35 MINUTES
PRESSURE LEVEL: HIGH • RELEASE: NATURAL

SERVES 4

4 tablespoons butter, divided

2 large leeks, soaked, rinsed, and chopped

3 garlic cloves, smashed

1½ pounds broccoli, cut into florets

3 cups vegetable or chicken broth

Kosher salt

Freshly ground black pepper

2 pinches red pepper flakes (optional)

3 tablespoons all-purpose flour

1 cup milk, plus more if needed

¼ cup grated Parmesan cheese, plus more for garnish

1. Preheat the Instant Pot by selecting Sauté.

2. Once hot, add 1 tablespoon of butter. Once melted, add the leeks and garlic and sauté for 5 minutes, or until the leeks are translucent.

3. Add the broccoli and broth, and season with salt and pepper. Add the red pepper flakes (if using). Secure the lid.

4. Select Manual and cook at high pressure for 6 minutes.

5. Meanwhile, in a small saucepan over medium-high heat, melt the remaining 3 tablespoons of butter on the stove. Whisk in the flour, followed by the milk. Cook, stirring, until thick and bubbly.

6. Once the pressure cooking is complete, use a natural release.

7. Add the Parmesan. Purée the broccoli and broth using an immersion blender or countertop blender. If using a countertop blender, blend in batches with the lid slightly cracked.

8. Return the broccoli mixture to the pot and add the milk mixture, stirring well. Taste for seasoning. If needed, select Sauté to reheat the soup.

9. Serve in bowls with a sprinkling of Parmesan on top.

INGREDIENT TIP: Leeks have pretty, overlapping leaves that like to hide sandy dirt. Soaking your leeks in cold water for about 30 minutes will help, followed by a good rinse.

Per Serving Calories: 294; Total Carbohydrates: 27g; Saturated Fat: 9g; Trans Fat: 0g; Fiber: 6g; Protein: 14g; Sodium: 853mg

One-Hour Matzo Ball Soup

Matzo ball soup always seems to be worth the time it takes to make, but wouldn't it be great if you could make it faster? With the help of a pressure cooker, you can have a deeply flavorful soup with tender matzo balls in an hour. This recipe utilizes premade broth, and you can make the matzo ball mixture up to a day ahead. The matzo balls are cooked separately from the broth to prevent a cloudy soup. I highly recommend using homemade broth for the best flavor.

PREP: 20 MINUTES, PLUS 30 MINUTES TO CHILL
PRESSURE: 20 MINUTES • TOTAL: 1 HOUR, 10 MINUTES
PRESSURE LEVEL: HIGH • RELEASE: QUICK, NATURAL

SERVES 4 TO 5

1 cup matzo meal, plus more if needed

⅛ teaspoon baking powder

1½ teaspoons kosher salt, divided, plus more for seasoning

¼ teaspoon freshly ground black pepper, plus more for seasoning

Pinch ground nutmeg

4 eggs

5¼ cups water, divided

¼ cup canola or vegetable oil

1 bone-in, skin-on chicken breast

1 bay leaf

6 cups homemade chicken broth (try the recipe on page 140)

1 large carrot, finely diced

2 celery stalks, finely diced

1 tablespoon chopped fresh dill (optional)

1. In a small bowl, combine the matzo meal, baking powder, 1 teaspoon of salt, pepper, and nutmeg.

2. In a medium bowl, beat together the eggs, ¼ cup of water, and the oil. Add the matzo mixture and mix well. The mixture will look like oatmeal. If it seems too soupy, add 1 tablespoon more matzo meal. Chill in the refrigerator for at least 30 minutes. The mixture will be easier to work with the longer it sits.

3. Meanwhile, add the chicken, 3 cups of water, the remaining ½ teaspoon salt, and the bay leaf to the Instant Pot. Select Manual and cook for 10 minutes at high pressure.

4. Once cooking is complete, select Cancel and use a quick release. Remove the chicken and set aside. Remove the bay leaf and discard.

5. Add water until the liquid in the Instant Pot reaches 5 cups (about 2 cups more water). Using a spoon and wet hands, form the matzo ball mixture into walnut-size balls (about 2 tablespoons). As you form them, set them on a plate. Once all of the balls are formed, carefully add them to the pot one at a time. ▶

One-Hour Matzo Ball Soup (continued)

6. Make sure the balls are all separated without disturbing them too much. Secure the lid.

7. Select Manual and cook at high pressure for 10 minutes.

8. Meanwhile, in a large pot on the stove, heat the broth to a low simmer. Add the carrot and celery and cook for 5 minutes. Season with salt and pepper and turn the heat to low.

9. Bone the chicken and discard the skin. Shred the meat.

10. Once the pressure cooking is complete, use a natural release.

11. Ladle the broth and veggies into bowls and add the chicken. Add 2 to 3 matzo balls per bowl and top with fresh dill (if using).

INGREDIENT TIP: You can easily make your own matzo meal using regular matzo. Simply break it into medium-size pieces and pulse it in your food processor until a cornmeal-like texture is reached. One sleeve of matzo typically yields 1 cup of meal.

Per Serving Calories: 456; Total Carbohydrates: 28g; Saturated Fat: 5g; Trans Fat: 0g; Fiber: 2g; Protein: 34g; Sodium: 2156mg

Vietnamese Chicken Noodle Soup *Pho Ga*

GLUTEN-FREE *In Vietnam, pho is eaten morning, noon, and night. The flavorful broth is traditionally cooked for hours to achieve a full-bodied flavor, but with a pressure cooker, you can enjoy this rich and complex soup in a fraction of the time.*

PREP: 10 MINUTES • PRESSURE: 15 MINUTES • TOTAL: 45 MINUTES
PRESSURE LEVEL: HIGH • RELEASE: NATURAL

SERVES 4

2 tablespoons canola oil

2 medium yellow onions, halved

1 (2-inch) piece ginger, cut into ¼-inch slices

1 tablespoon coriander seeds

3 star anise pods

5 cloves

1 cinnamon stick

3 cardamom pods, lightly smashed

6 bone-in, skin-on chicken thighs

3 tablespoons fish sauce

1 tablespoon sugar

8 cups water

Kosher salt

Freshly ground black pepper

4 servings rice noodles, prepared according to package directions

Toppings

3 scallions, sliced

1 small handful fresh herbs, such as mint, cilantro, and Thai basil, chopped

1 lime, cut into wedges

Handful of bean sprouts (optional)

1 jalapeño, thinly sliced (optional)

1. Preheat the Instant Pot by selecting Sauté on high heat.

2. Once hot, add the oil to the pot. Add the onions, cut-side down, and the ginger. Cook, without moving, until charred—about 4 minutes.

3. Add the coriander, star anise, cloves, cinnamon stick, and cardamom. Stir and cook for 1 minute more. Add the chicken, fish sauce, and sugar and immediately pour over the water. Secure the lid.

4. Select Manual and cook at high pressure for 15 minutes.

5. Once cooking is complete, use a natural release for 10 minutes and release any remaining steam. Remove the chicken from the pot and carefully strain the broth. Season with salt and pepper as desired.

6. Place the cooked noodles in 4 bowls. When the chicken is cool enough to handle, pick the meat off the bones and add to the bowls. Pour over the broth and top with scallions, herbs, lime, and bean sprouts and jalapeño (if using).

INGREDIENT TIP: If you have trouble finding whole dried spices, try your local international market or health food store, or order them online.

Per Serving Calories: 620; Total Carbohydrates: 57g; Saturated Fat: 8g; Trans Fat: 0g; Fiber: 4g; Protein: 25g; Sodium: 1220mg

French Onion Soup

French onion soup seems a lot harder to make than it actually is. The onions are caramelized in the Instant Pot and then cooked with savory broth. A topping of toast and Gruyère cheese turns this simple soup into a decadent dish.

PREP: 30 MINUTES • PRESSURE: 6 MINUTES • TOTAL: 45 MINUTES
PRESSURE LEVEL: HIGH • RELEASE: QUICK

SERVES 4 TO 5

5 tablespoons butter

2 pounds yellow and/or sweet onions, cut into ⅛-inch slices

Kosher salt

Freshly ground black pepper

Pinch sugar

½ cup dry white wine

6 cups beef or chicken broth, preferably homemade (try the recipes on pages 142 and 140)

2 fresh thyme sprigs

1 loaf French bread, cut into ¾-inch slices and toasted (enough to cover the top of 4 or 5 bowls)

1 cup grated Gruyère cheese

1. Preheat the Instant Pot by selecting Sauté. Add the butter.

2. Once the butter has melted, add the onions and stir. Cover loosely with the lid and cook, stirring occasionally, until translucent, about 15 minutes.

3. Lower the heat to low. Season with salt and pepper and add the sugar. Cook, stirring frequently, until the onions turn golden brown and become translucent, about 10 minutes.

4. Raise the heat back to medium. Add the wine, scrape off any brown bits from the bottom of the pot, and let most of the wine evaporate.

5. Add the broth and thyme and season with salt and pepper. Secure the lid.

6. Select Manual and cook at high pressure for 6 minutes.

7. Once cooking is complete, use a quick release.

8. Preheat the oven to broil.

9. Spoon the soup into ovenproof bowls and top with toasted bread. Sprinkle the top with cheese and place under the broiler for 5 to 7 minutes until the cheese is bubbly.

COOKING TIP: This soup is great for making ahead. Make the soup through step 7, then cool and freeze or refrigerate. To serve, reheat it on the stove and then proceed with the recipe as written.

Per Serving Calories: 598; Total Carbohydrates: 59g; Saturated Fat: 15g; Trans Fat: 0g; Fiber: 7g; Protein: 23g; Sodium: 1864mg

Butternut Squash and Sausage Soup with Crispy Sage

GLUTEN-FREE, PALEO-FRIENDLY *Butternut squash soup is perfect for fall, but it tastes great all year long. Sausage pairs nicely with the lightly sweet and creamy soup, and fried sage adds an herby crunch. The baking soda helps the squash magically brown in the pot, giving the soup a stronger flavor.*

PREP: 12 MINUTES • PRESSURE: 15 MINUTES • TOTAL: 35 MINUTES
PRESSURE LEVEL: HIGH • RELEASE: QUICK

SERVES 4

2 tablespoons extra-virgin olive oil

8 fresh sage leaves

10 ounces uncooked Italian-style pork or chicken sausage, without casing

½ large yellow onion, chopped

2 small celery stalks, chopped

2 large garlic cloves, smashed

1 medium butternut squash, peeled, seeded, and cut into 1-inch cubes (about 4 cups)

2 cups chicken or vegetable broth, plus more as needed

½ teaspoon baking soda

Kosher salt

Freshly ground black pepper

½ cup heavy cream or half-and-half (optional)

Pinch ground nutmeg

1. To preheat the Instant Pot, select Sauté on high. Once hot, add the oil followed by the sage leaves. Fry for 2 to 3 minutes until crispy. Remove and drain on a paper towel.

2. Add the sausage. Use a spoon or spatula to break up the sausage into small pieces as it cooks. Continue until the sausage is cooked through. Use a slotted spoon to transfer the sausage to a plate.

3. Add the onion to the pot and cook for 1 minute. Add the celery and garlic and cook, stirring occasionally, for about 3 minutes, or until the onion is translucent and lightly browned.

4. Add the squash, broth, and baking soda and stir. Season with salt and pepper. Secure the lid.

5. Select Manual and cook at high pressure for 15 minutes.

6. Once cooking is complete, use a quick release.

7. Add the cream (if using) and nutmeg, and purée with an immersion blender. Alternatively, blend in batches in a blender with the lid slightly cracked. Add more broth or cream if you want a thinner soup. Taste for seasoning. Serve in bowls topped with crispy sage.

SUBSTITUTION TIP: To make this dish Paleo, leave out the cream and substitute with more broth.

Per Serving Calories: 536; Total Carbohydrates: 26g; Saturated Fat: 5g; Trans Fat: 0g; Fiber: 3g; Protein: 29g; Sodium: 261mg

Sweet Potato, Sausage, and Kale Soup

GLUTEN-FREE *Sweet potatoes are high in fiber and nutrients, and kale is a bona fide superfood. They come together with the help of flavorful sausage to make a wholesome, meal-in-a-bowl soup. Kielbasa works great, but any hard sausage of a similar style works, including Portuguese linguiça or Spanish chorizo.*

PREP: 20 MINUTES • PRESSURE: 8 MINUTES • TOTAL: 45 MINUTES
PRESSURE LEVEL: HIGH • RELEASE: NATURAL

SERVES 6 TO 8

2 tablespoons extra-virgin olive oil

1 (10-ounce) fully cooked kielbasa, linguiça, or Spanish chorizo, cut into ¼-inch slices

1 large onion, chopped

3 garlic cloves, minced

2 pounds sweet potatoes, peeled and cut into 1-inch cubes

1 pound Yukon Gold or white potatoes (not russets), peeled and cut into 1-inch cubes

6 cups chicken broth

Kosher salt

Freshly ground black pepper

1 small bunch kale, stemmed and roughly chopped

1. Preheat the Instant Pot by selecting Sauté.

2. Once hot, add the oil followed by the sausage. Cook, stirring, for about 7 minutes, until browned. Remove and place on paper towels to drain.

3. Add the onion and garlic. Cook for 5 minutes, or until the onion is translucent.

4. Add the sweet potatoes, potatoes, and broth. Season with salt and pepper. Secure the lid.

5. Select Manual and cook at high pressure for 8 minutes.

6. Once cooking is complete, select Cancel and use a natural release for 10 minutes and then release any remaining steam.

7. Use a potato masher or immersion blender to mash about half of the potatoes, leaving some chunks.

8. Select Sauté and add the kale. Cook for 5 minutes more until the kale is wilted. Add the sausage and serve.

INSTANT POT TIP: The Soup setting can be used for this recipe. When you're ready to pressure-cook, select Soup and set the timer for 8 minutes. Proceed with the recipe as written.

Per Serving Calories: 450; Total Carbohydrates: 64g; Saturated Fat: 4g; Trans Fat: 0g; Fiber: 9g; Protein: 16g; Sodium: 1396mg

Lentil and Spinach Stew with Shrimp

GLUTEN-FREE *A hearty lentil stew is brightened by plump shrimp and vibrant spinach added at the last minute. Use good-quality chicken broth for best results, and leave out the shrimp if you must—it's still a great soup, especially served with crusty bread.*

PREP: 10 MINUTES • PRESSURE: 20 MINUTES • TOTAL: 45 MINUTES
PRESSURE LEVEL: HIGH • RELEASE: NATURAL

SERVES 4

2 tablespoons extra-virgin olive oil

1 small onion, chopped

2 carrots, peeled and chopped

2 celery stalks, chopped

4 garlic cloves, minced

½ teaspoon ground cumin

¼ teaspoon ground turmeric

3 cups chicken broth (try the recipe on page 140)

1 cup dried green lentils, rinsed and drained

1 bay leaf

Kosher salt

Freshly ground black pepper

16 uncooked large shrimp, peeled and deveined

5 ounces fresh spinach, roughly chopped

Juice of ½ lemon

1. Preheat the Instant Pot by selecting Sauté.

2. Once hot, add the oil, onion, carrots, celery, and garlic. Cook for 3 minutes, or until the onion is beginning to turn translucent.

3. Add the cumin and turmeric and stir. Add the broth, lentils, and bay leaf. Season with salt and pepper. Secure the lid.

4. Select Manual and cook at high pressure for 20 minutes.

5. Once cooking is complete, use a natural release for 10 minutes and release any remaining steam.

6. Select Sauté. Add the shrimp and spinach to the pot and stir. Once the soup starts boiling, turn the heat off. Let it sit for a few minutes until the shrimp are opaque.

7. Remove and discard the bay leaf. Add the lemon juice. Serve in bowls.

INSTANT POT TIP: The Soup setting can be used for this recipe. Select Soup and set the timer to 20 minutes.

Per Serving Calories: 675; Total Carbohydrates: 96g; Saturated Fat: 6g; Trans Fat: 0g; Fiber: 14g; Protein: 25g; Sodium: 2096mg

Beef Stew with Mushrooms and Barley

This hearty beef stew is a complete meal, thanks to a dose of fresh mushrooms and wholesome barley. Rather than cook on the stove for hours, this flavorful dish is ready in an hour and only requires one pot. Add more liquid at the end if the stew is too thick for your liking.

**PREP: 15 MINUTES • PRESSURE: 25 MINUTES • TOTAL: 1 HOUR
PRESSURE LEVEL: HIGH • RELEASE: NATURAL**

1. Preheat the Instant Pot by selecting Sauté on high heat. Add the oil to the pot.

2. Season the beef with salt and pepper and coat in the flour. Shake off the excess.

3. Once hot, add half of the beef and let it sit in the pot to brown for about 3 minutes. Turn and brown the other side. Remove and repeat with the rest of the beef. Set aside.

4. Add the onion to the pot, stir, and cook for 4 minutes until lightly browned. Add the mushrooms and stir. Add the wine and deglaze the pot by scraping the bottom to remove all of the brown bits.

5. Add the carrots, celery, garlic, rosemary, thyme, bay leaf, broth, water, barley, and beef. Season with salt and pepper. Stir and secure the lid.

6. Select Manual and cook on high pressure for 25 minutes.

7. Once cooking is complete, use a natural release. Serve in bowls or on soup plates.

SUBSTITUTION TIP: If you don't have any red wine, use white wine or vermouth to deglaze the pan—but red wine provides the best flavor.

Per Serving Calories: 521; Total Carbohydrates: 37g; Saturated Fat: 4g; Trans Fat: 0g; Fiber: 7g; Protein: 54g; Sodium: 534mg

SERVES 6

2 tablespoons canola oil

2 pounds stewing beef (chuck, round, or rump roast), trimmed of fat and cut into 1-inch cubes

Kosher salt

Freshly ground black pepper

¼ cup all-purpose flour

1 onion, diced

8 ounces mushrooms, chopped

½ cup dry red wine

2 carrots, peeled and chopped

2 celery stalks, chopped

3 garlic cloves, minced

1 small fresh rosemary sprig

3 fresh thyme sprigs

1 bay leaf

3 cups beef broth

1 cup water

1 cup pearl barley

Tuscan Chicken Stew

GLUTEN-FREE *With little more to do than throw the ingredients in the pressure cooker and retrieve the finished product 20 minutes later, this is as simple as stew gets. It's more substantial than your average soup, brightly flavored, and begging to be sopped up with crusty bread. Customize it as you see fit. Don't like beans? Leave them out. Want more broth? Pour more in there.*

PREP: 10 MINUTES • PRESSURE: 10 MINUTES • TOTAL: 40 MINUTES
PRESSURE LEVEL: HIGH • RELEASE: NATURAL

1. Preheat the Instant Pot by selecting Sauté.

2. Once hot, add the oil. Add the onion, celery, and carrots and stir. Cook for 5 minutes until the onion is translucent. Add the garlic and cook for 1 minute more.

3. Add the potatoes, tomatoes with juice, beans, broth, chicken, oregano, and red pepper flakes. Season with salt and pepper and mix gently.

4. Select Manual and cook at high pressure for 10 minutes.

5. Once cooking is complete, use a natural release. This will take 10 to 15 minutes.

6. Remove the chicken and pull the meat off the bones. Return the meat to the pot and add the vinegar and parsley. Taste for seasoning and serve.

INSTANT POT TIP: The Soup setting can be used for this recipe. Select Soup and set the timer to 10 minutes. Proceed with the recipe as written.

Per Serving Calories: 352; Total Carbohydrates: 42g; Saturated Fat: 2g; Trans Fat: 0g; Fiber: 12g; Protein: 23g; Sodium: 457mg

SERVES 4 TO 5

2 tablespoons extra-virgin olive oil

1 onion, chopped

2 celery stalks, chopped

2 carrots, peeled and chopped

4 garlic cloves, minced

1 pound small red or white potatoes, halved

1 (14.5-ounce) can chopped or crushed tomatoes with juice

1 (15-ounce) can red kidney beans, rinsed and drained

1 cup chicken broth

6 bone-in, skin-on chicken thighs and/or drumsticks

1 teaspoon dried oregano

Large pinch red pepper flakes

Kosher salt

Freshly ground black pepper

1 tablespoon balsamic vinegar

2 tablespoons chopped fresh parsley leaves

Lightning-Fast Veggie Chili

VEGETARIAN *Meaty chilies need some time to stew and break down, but a meat-free, bean-based chili can be ready in 20 minutes thanks to canned beans. Include the jalapeño and an extra teaspoon of chili powder if you like spice. Serve with tortilla chips or cornbread.*

PREP: 5 MINUTES • PRESSURE: 3 MINUTES • TOTAL: 20 MINUTES
PRESSURE LEVEL: HIGH • RELEASE: QUICK

1. To preheat the Instant Pot, select Sauté.

2. Once hot, add the oil. Add the garlic, scallions (reserving 2 tablespoons of greens), bell pepper, and jalapeño (if using). Stir and sauté for 3 minutes, until the veggies begin to soften.

3. Add the chili powder, cumin, salt, and pepper. Stir and cook for 1 minute until fragrant.

4. Add the black beans, pinto or kidney beans, tomatoes with juice, corn, and beer or water. Secure the lid.

5. Select Manual and cook at high pressure for 3 minutes.

6. Once cooking is complete, use a quick release. Carefully remove the lid and stir.

7. If a thicker chili is desired, select Sauté and cook on high heat for 3 to 5 minutes. Season as desired.

8. Serve in bowls with a dollop of sour cream (if using), a sprinkle of the reserved chopped green scallions, and tortilla chips.

VARIATION TIP: Switch out the beans to your liking—white beans and even chickpeas work.

Per Serving Calories: 410; Total Carbohydrates: 67g; Saturated Fat: 1g; Trans Fat: 0g; Fiber: 20g; Protein: 21g; Sodium: 659mg

SERVES 4

1 tablespoon extra-virgin olive oil

3 garlic cloves, minced

12 scallions, whites and greens chopped, with 2 tablespoons chopped greens reserved

1 bell pepper, diced

1 jalapeño, finely diced (optional)

2 teaspoons chili powder

1 teaspoon ground cumin

½ teaspoon kosher salt

¼ teaspoon freshly ground black pepper

2 (15-ounce) cans black beans, rinsed and drained

1 (15-ounce) can pinto or kidney beans, rinsed and drained

1 (14.5-ounce) can diced tomatoes with juice, with or without chiles

1 cup frozen corn

½ cup beer (preferably lager) or water

Sour cream, for serving (optional)

Tortilla chips, for serving

Chorizo Chili

GLUTEN-FREE *A two-part cook time ensures perfectly cooked pinto beans. Fresh Mexican chorizo—not to be confused with smoked Spanish chorizo—is typically found in the supermarket meat section or at Mexican markets. Serve with toppings like shredded cheese, sour cream, and scallions.*

PREP: 10 MINUTES • PRESSURE: 23 MINUTES • TOTAL: 1 HOUR, 5 MINUTES • PRESSURE LEVEL: HIGH • RELEASE: NATURAL

SERVES 8

2 tablespoons canola oil, divided

2 cups dried pinto beans, rinsed, picked over (discard any bad beans), and soaked overnight

6 cups water

8 ounces Mexican chorizo, without casing

12 ounces ground beef

1 large onion, chopped

1 large red bell pepper, chopped

1 large jalapeño, seeded and minced

3 garlic cloves, minced

1 tablespoon unsweetened cocoa powder

2 teaspoons ground cumin

1½ teaspoons chili powder

1 teaspoon dried oregano

1 (14.5-ounce) can diced tomatoes with juice

Kosher salt

Freshly ground black pepper

1. Add 1 tablespoon of oil, the beans, and water to the Instant Pot. Select Manual and cook at high pressure for 13 minutes.

2. When cooking is complete, select Cancel and use a natural release.

3. Drain the beans, reserving 2 cups of cooking liquid. Rinse and dry the pot.

4. Select Sauté on high heat and add the remaining 1 table-spoon of oil. Add the chorizo and beef and break up with a wooden spoon or spatula. Cook until mostly browned, about 4 minutes, and add the onion. Stir and cook for 2 minutes more.

5. Add the bell pepper, jalapeño, and garlic. Stir and cook for 2 minutes. Add the cocoa, cumin, chili powder, and oregano and stir. Cook for 1 minute.

6. Add the diced tomatoes with juice, beans, and reserved cooking liquid. Stir and season with salt and pepper. Secure the lid.

7. Select Manual and cook at high pressure for 10 minutes.

8. Once cooking is complete, select Cancel and use a natural release. Serve.

INGREDIENT TIP: If you didn't soak your beans, simply add 15 minutes to the cook time of the beans and proceed with the recipe as written.

Per Serving Calories: 374; Total Carbohydrates: 38g; Saturated Fat: 3g; Trans Fat: 0g; Fiber: 10g; Protein: 33g; Sodium: 246mg

CHAPTER SIX
SEAFOOD AND POULTRY

≈≈≈≈≈≈≈≈≈≈≈≈≈≈≈

Mussels with Shallots and White Wine

GLUTEN-FREE, PALEO-FRIENDLY *Mussels cook effortlessly to perfection in a bath of white wine, shallots, garlic, and lemon in just three minutes. Top with fresh parsley and serve with crusty bread and more wine (of course).*

PREP: 10 MINUTES • PRESSURE: 3 MINUTES • TOTAL: 20 MINUTES
PRESSURE LEVEL: LOW • RELEASE: QUICK

SERVES 4

2 pounds fresh mussels

1 tablespoon extra-virgin olive oil

3 large shallots, minced

2 garlic cloves, minced

½ cup dry white wine

½ cup chicken broth or water

Pinch red pepper flakes (optional)

Juice of ½ lemon

Fresh parsley or dill, chopped, for garnish

1. Clean the mussels using a dry brush and cold water. De-beard them as needed by grasping the thin membrane on the back of each mussel and pulling it off. Discard any mussels that don't close after being tapped a few times against another mussel.

2. To preheat the Instant Pot, select Sauté.

3. Once hot, add the oil, shallots, and garlic. Cook, stirring, for 2 minutes.

4. Add the mussels, wine, broth or water, and red pepper flakes (if using).

5. Secure the top and select Manual. Cook at low pressure for 3 minutes.

6. Once cooking is complete, use a quick release. Top with the lemon juice and fresh parsley. Serve with the broth.

SUBSTITUTION TIP: To make this recipe Paleo, replace the wine with more broth.

Per Serving Calories: 262; Total Carbohydrates: 11g; Saturated Fat: 2g; Trans Fat: 0g; Fiber: 0g; Protein: 28g; Sodium: 747mg

Crab Legs with Lemon and Garlic Butter Sauce

GLUTEN-FREE *Perfectly steamed crab legs are just a few minutes away. Using the Instant Pot ensures even, fast cooking, and the butter is flavored with garlic and lemon for a bright sauce. Serve alongside crusty bread, a salad, and corn on the cob for a seaside feast.*

PREP: 3 MINUTES • PRESSURE: 3 MINUTES • TOTAL: 15 MINUTES
PRESSURE LEVEL: HIGH • RELEASE: QUICK

SERVES 4

1 cup water

2 pounds fresh or frozen crab legs

1 teaspoon extra-virgin olive oil

1 large garlic clove, minced

4 tablespoons salted butter

1 lemon, halved

1. Prepare the Instant Pot by adding the water and placing a steamer basket on top.

2. Add the crab legs and secure the lid.

3. Select Steam and cook at high pressure for 3 minutes. If using frozen crab, cook for 4 minutes.

4. While the crab is steaming, heat the oil over medium heat in a small saucepan. Add the garlic and cook, stirring, for 1 minute. Don't let the garlic burn.

5. Add the butter and melt. Stir and turn off the heat. Add a big squeeze of lemon.

6. Once the pressure cooking is complete, use a quick release.

7. Serve the crab legs on a platter with the butter dipping sauce on the side.

COOKING TIP: A metal steamer basket works best for this and some other recipes in this book. Before purchasing one, make sure it fits in the pot.

Per Serving Calories: 346; Total Carbohydrates: 2g; Saturated Fat: 7g; Trans Fat: 0g; Fiber: 0g; Protein: 44g; Sodium: 2510mg

Low-Country Boil

GLUTEN-FREE *If you've never had a low-country boil, then you've been missing out. The southern coastal dish incorporates potatoes, sausage, corn on the cob, and shellfish in such a way that they're all done cooking at the same time. It's traditionally drained and all dumped out on a table lined with newspaper for everyone to feast on.*

PREP: 5 MINUTES • PRESSURE: 9 MINUTES • TOTAL: 35 MINUTES
PRESSURE LEVEL: HIGH • RELEASE: QUICK

1. Add the water, seasoning packet, salt, and lemon to the Instant Pot. Add the potatoes and sausage and secure the lid.

2. Select Manual and cook at high pressure for 7 minutes.

3. Once cooking is complete, use a quick release. Add the corn and secure the lid.

4. Select Manual and cook at high pressure for 1 minute.

5. When cooking is complete, use a quick release. Add the shrimp and secure the lid.

6. Select Manual and cook at high pressure for 1 minute.

7. Once cooking is complete, use a quick release.

8. Drain and season with salt as needed.

INGREDIENT TIP: If you can't find boil-in-bag seafood seasoning packets, then add ½ to 1 teaspoon seafood seasoning per cup of water.

Per Serving Calories: 640; Total Carbohydrates: 43g; Saturated Fat: 7g; Trans Fat: 0g; Fiber: 5g; Protein: 68g; Sodium: 4501mg

SERVES 4 TO 5

8 cups water

1 (3-ounce) boil-in-bag seafood seasoning packet

1½ tablespoons kosher salt, plus more for seasoning

1 lemon, halved

1½ pounds baby red new potatoes

1 pound mild or hot smoked sausage (like kielbasa), cut into 3 or 4 pieces each

3 ears corn, shucked, and halved

2 pounds uncooked medium shrimp, unpeeled

Shrimp Scampi

GLUTEN-FREE *For shrimp lovers, a little garlic, white wine, and butter are all that's needed to enjoy the shellfish. Shrimp scampi is brilliant in its simplicity, and is lovely served with its sauce over pasta or another grain. It also makes a nice appetizer.*

PREP: 5 MINUTES • PRESSURE: 1 MINUTE • TOTAL: 20 MINUTES
PRESSURE LEVEL: HIGH • RELEASE: QUICK

SERVES 4

2 tablespoons butter

3 large garlic cloves, minced

¼ cup dry white wine

½ cup chicken broth

1 pound uncooked large shrimp, shelled and deveined

Kosher salt

Freshly ground black pepper

Juice of ½ lemon

1 heaping teaspoon chopped fresh parsley

1. Preheat the Instant Pot by selecting Sauté.

2. Once hot, add the butter. Once the butter has melted, add the garlic and cook, stirring, for 1 minute. Add the wine and cook for 2 minutes, or until the smell of alcohol goes away.

3. Add the broth and the shrimp, and season with salt and pepper. Secure the lid.

4. Select Manual and cook at high pressure for 1 minute.

5. Once cooking is complete, use a quick release. Remove the shrimp. Select Sauté on high heat and cook for 2 minutes more to reduce the sauce.

6. Add the lemon juice and parsley and stir. Serve.

INGREDIENT TIP: High-quality frozen shrimp will also work—just add 1 minute to the pressure cooking time.

Per Serving Calories: 162; Total Carbohydrates: 3g; Saturated Fat: 4g; Trans Fat: 0g; Fiber: 0g; Protein: 22g; Sodium: 318mg

Steamed Fish and Veggies

GLUTEN-FREE, PALEO-FRIENDLY *Because most fish is so easy to overcook, it isn't always the best thing to prepare in a pressure cooker. However, it is possible to make great fish with your Instant Pot. This healthy dish emulates steaming fish in a packet with the vegetables and aromatics adding depth.*

PREP: 10 MINUTES • PRESSURE: 5 MINUTES • TOTAL: 25 MINUTES
PRESSURE LEVEL: LOW • RELEASE: QUICK

1. Preheat the Instant Pot by selecting Sauté.

2. Once hot, add the oil. Add the onion and cook for 2 minutes until it is beginning to turn translucent. Add the garlic and cook, stirring, for 1 minute more.

3. Add the tomatoes and zucchini and stir, cooking for 1 minute until some juice has released. Add the fish on top, along with the broth, lemon, thyme, and saffron (if using), and season with salt and pepper. Secure the lid.

4. Select Manual and cook at low pressure for 5 minutes.

5. Once cooking is complete, use a quick release. Serve the vegetables topped with the fish and a slice of lemon.

INGREDIENT TIP: If using frozen fish, add 2 minutes to the pressure-cook time.

Per Serving Calories: 406; Total Carbohydrates: 24g; Saturated Fat: 3g; Trans Fat: 0g; Fiber: 7; Protein: 43g; Sodium: 213mg

SERVES 4

1 tablespoon extra-virgin olive oil

1 small onion, cut into ⅛-inch slices

3 garlic cloves, minced

16 cherry tomatoes, halved

1 cup chopped zucchini or summer squash

4 small white fish fillets (such as cod)

¼ cup vegetable, chicken, or fish broth

1 lemon, cut into ¼-inch rounds

3 fresh thyme sprigs

Small pinch saffron (optional)

Kosher salt

Freshly ground black pepper

Green Chicken Enchiladas

GLUTEN-FREE *This is Mexican comfort food at its best—tender chicken rolled up inside tortillas, napped with a mild green enchilada sauce, and topped with melted cheese. It's an easy recipe you'll be asked to make time and time again.*

PREP: 10 MINUTES • PRESSURE: 7 MINUTES • TOTAL: 45 MINUTES
PRESSURE LEVEL: HIGH • RELEASE: QUICK

SERVES 4

3 medium boneless, skinless chicken breasts

Kosher salt

Freshly ground black pepper

1 cup chicken broth or water

2 garlic cloves, minced

½ onion, sliced

2 (10-ounce) cans green enchilada sauce, divided

½ cup sour cream, plus more for serving

10 to 12 corn tortillas

2 cups Monterey Jack cheese

1. Season the chicken with salt and pepper and place it in the Instant Pot, along with the broth, garlic, and onion. Secure the lid.

2. Select Manual and cook at high pressure for 7 minutes.

3. Preheat the oven to 375°F.

4. Once pressure cooking is complete, use a quick release. Remove the chicken, shred it, and combine in a large bowl with ½ cup of enchilada sauce and the sour cream. Season with salt and pepper.

5. Spread another ½ cup of enchilada sauce into a 9-by-13-inch baking dish. Warm the tortillas slightly in the oven, on the stove, or in the microwave to make them pliable. Fill each with 2 to 3 tablespoons of the chicken mixture and a sprinkle of cheese. Roll into cigar shapes and place, side-by-side and seam-side down, into the baking dish.

6. Top with the remaining sauce and cheese. Cover with foil.

7. Bake for 15 minutes. Remove the foil and bake for 5 to 10 minutes more, until the cheese is melted. Serve hot.

INSTANT POT TIP: The chicken can also be cooked using the Slow Cook setting. Combine the chicken, ½ cup enchilada sauce, 1½ cups broth, garlic, onion, and sour cream in the pot. Slow Cook for 6 to 8 hours and proceed with the recipe as written.

Per Serving Calories: 669; Total Carbohydrates: 37g; Saturated Fat: 17g; Trans Fat: 0g; Fiber: 5g; Protein: 51g; Sodium: 1600mg

Chicken Pot Pie

Squares of oven-browned, store-bought puff pastry replace the traditional pot pie crust, topping this classic before serving. It's a surprisingly easy meal that's fit for company.

WEEKDAY WIN • FAMILY-FRIENDLY

PREP: 20 MINUTES • PRESSURE: 7 MINUTES • TOTAL: 45 MINUTES
PRESSURE LEVEL: HIGH • RELEASE: QUICK

1. Thaw the puff pastry sheet on the counter for 30 minutes.

2. Preheat the oven to 400°F.

3. Select Sauté on the Instant Pot and add the oil.

4. Add the onion, carrots, and celery. Stir and cook for 3 minutes, until the onion starts to turn translucent. Add the potatoes, chicken, broth, and salt. Secure the lid.

5. Select Manual and cook at high pressure for 7 minutes.

6. Meanwhile, once the pastry sheet is pliable but still cold, lay it out on a baking sheet and cut into 4 even squares or rectangles. Bake for 15 minutes.

7. Once pressure cooking is complete, use a quick release. Remove the chicken and, once cool enough to handle, pull off the meat and discard the skin and bones. Cut the meat into cubes.

8. Select Sauté on the pot.

SERVES 4 TO 5

1 frozen puff pastry sheet

1 tablespoon extra-virgin olive oil

1 small onion, chopped

2 medium carrots, peeled and chopped

2 celery stalks, chopped

2 medium potatoes, cut into ¾-inch cubes

3 medium bone-in, skin-on chicken breasts

1½ cups chicken broth

1 teaspoon kosher salt

2 tablespoons all-purpose flour

2 tablespoons cold butter

½ cup heavy cream or whole milk

1 cup frozen peas

Freshly ground black pepper

9. In a small bowl, combine the flour and butter into a smooth paste. Add the paste to the simmering broth along with the cream or milk and peas. Cook, stirring, until the paste has dissolved, 3 to 5 minutes. Add the chicken and season with salt and pepper.

10. To serve, spoon the stew into bowls and top with the puff pastry.

INGREDIENT TIP: If you're using chicken broth that's salty, you may need to decrease the amount of salt. I recommend always buying low-salt broth, or making it from scratch at home (try the recipe on page 140).

Per Serving Calories: 738; Total Carbohydrates: 58g; Saturated Fat: 14g; Trans Fat: 0g; Fiber: 7g; Protein: 30g; Sodium: 1459mg

Greek-Style Chicken with Potatoes and Peas

GLUTEN-FREE *This quick, crispy-skinned chicken is flavored with garlic, olive oil, spices, and lemon. Potatoes cook right along with the chicken, and peas and olives are added at the last minute, making it a complete meal.*

PREP: 10 MINUTES • PRESSURE: 7 MINUTES • TOTAL: 1 HOUR
PRESSURE LEVEL: HIGH • RELEASE: NATURAL

SERVES 4

4 small or 3 large bone-in, skin-on chicken breasts

Kosher salt

Freshly ground black pepper

4 tablespoons extra-virgin olive oil, divided, plus extra for garnish

3 garlic cloves, minced

1 fresh rosemary sprig, chopped (leaves only)

1 teaspoon dried oregano

Pinch red pepper flakes

1 pound large fingerling potatoes, washed and pricked with a knife

2 cups chicken broth

1 cup frozen peas

1 lemon

½ cup olives

1. Season the chicken with salt and pepper. In a large bowl, coat the chicken with 2 tablespoons of olive oil, the garlic, rosemary, oregano, and red pepper flakes. Marinate for at least 30 minutes in the refrigerator.

2. To preheat the Instant Pot, select Sauté on high heat.

3. When hot, add the remaining 2 tablespoons of olive oil and coat the bottom of the pot. Add the chicken, skin-side down (reserving any marinade), and cook without moving for about 5 minutes, until the skin is crispy. Remove the chicken and select Cancel.

4. Add the potatoes and broth. Place the chicken on top, skin-side up, and pour the reserved marinade on top. Season with salt and pepper and secure the lid.

5. Select Manual and cook at high pressure for 7 minutes.

6. Once cooking is complete, use a natural release for 10 minutes and then release any remaining pressure.

7. Remove the chicken. Stir in the peas and cook until warmed.

8. Serve the potatoes and peas topped with the chicken. Just before serving, add a squeeze of lemon, a drizzle of olive oil, and the olives.

INGREDIENT TIP: Fresh peas also work for this recipe, and a sprinkle of chopped fresh mint adds a new layer of flavor.

Per Serving Calories: 388; Total Carbohydrates: 26g; Saturated Fat: 5g; Trans Fat: 0g; Fiber: 5g; Protein: 25g; Sodium: 794mg

Classic Chicken Wings

GLUTEN-FREE, PALEO-FRIENDLY *You'll wow everyone on the next game day when you whip up these wings. The pressure cooker quickly cooks the chicken wings until tender before they're fried or broiled, depending on your preference. Use your favorite sauce, such as barbecue, buffalo, or teriyaki.*

PREP: 5 MINUTES • PRESSURE: 10 MINUTES
TOTAL: 40 MINUTES (IF BROILING) OR 1 HOUR, 40 MINUTES
(IF FRYING) • PRESSURE LEVEL: HIGH • RELEASE: NATURAL

SERVES 4 TO 5

3 pounds chicken wings

1 cup water

Kosher salt

2 cups wing sauce

8 to 10 cups vegetable oil
(depending on the size of
your pot), if frying

1. Add the chicken wings and water to the Instant Pot and season with salt. Secure the lid.

2. Select Manual and cook at high pressure for 10 minutes.

3. Once cooking is complete, use a natural release for 10 minutes and then release any remaining pressure. Remove the wings to a cooling rack to drain.

4. To broil the wings: Preheat the oven to broil. In a large bowl, toss the wings in the sauce. Place on a baking sheet and broil for about 5 minutes, until crispy. Flip the wings and repeat.

5. To fry the wings: Place the cooling rack with the wings on a baking sheet and refrigerate for 1 hour.

6. In a large pot or Dutch oven, heat the oil to 385°F (use a cooking thermometer).

7. Once hot, carefully lower 7 or 8 wings into the oil and fry for 3 minutes until crispy. Remove and place back on the rack. Repeat with the remaining wings.

8. Toss the wings in the sauce and serve immediately.

COOKING TIP: Refrigerating the wings before frying ensures that they are dry, making them easier to fry.

Per Serving Calories: 746; Total Carbohydrates: 8g; Saturated Fat: 7g; Trans Fat: 0g; Fiber: 0g; Protein: 98g; Sodium: 2091mg

Chicken and Dumplings

This Southern classic is stick-to-your-ribs food. The combination of flavorful chicken, creamy broth, and tender dumplings is comforting and filling. Don't be scared to make your own dumplings—they're easier than you think! Be careful not to overwork the dough, since it will quickly become tough. Add finely chopped herbs to your dumplings, if you have them, for a bit of freshness.

PREP: 20 MINUTES • PRESSURE: 11 MINUTES • TOTAL: 55 MINUTES
PRESSURE LEVEL: HIGH • RELEASE: QUICK

SERVES 8

For the chicken and broth

4 tablespoons butter

8 medium bone-in, skin-on chicken thighs

Kosher salt

Freshly ground black pepper

½ cup all-purpose flour

4 celery stalks, chopped

3 carrots, peeled and chopped

2 onions, chopped

3½ cups chicken broth, preferably homemade (try the recipe on page 140)

½ cup whole milk or half-and-half

2 tablespoons cornstarch

For the dumplings

1¾ cups all-purpose flour

¼ cup cornmeal

1 tablespoon baking powder

½ teaspoon kosher salt

¼ teaspoon freshly ground black pepper

1 cup whole milk or half-and-half

3 tablespoons melted butter

To make the chicken and broth

1. Preheat the Instant Pot by selecting Sauté on high heat. Add the butter.

2. Season the chicken with salt and pepper and dredge in the flour, shaking off the excess. Once the butter is sizzling and the pot is hot, add half of the chicken in one layer. Brown on one side for 3 or 4 minutes, without moving, and flip and brown on the other side. Remove and repeat with the remaining chicken. Set aside.

3. Add the celery, carrots, and onions to the pot. Sauté for 3 minutes, scraping the bottom of the pot. Add the chicken and broth. Season with salt and pepper. Secure the lid.

4. Select Manual and cook at high pressure for 11 minutes.

To make the dumplings

1. While the chicken is cooking, make the dumplings. Mix together the flour, cornmeal, baking powder, salt, and pepper in a medium bowl. Add the milk or half-and-half and melted butter, and stir just until incorporated (don't over-mix). Set aside.

2. Once cooking is complete, use a quick release. Remove the chicken and set aside.

3. Add the milk to the broth in the pot, mix, and season with salt and pepper. In a small bowl, combine ½ cup of hot broth with the cornstarch and whisk well to combine. Add back to the pot and stir.

4. Select Sauté. Once simmering, scoop heaping tablespoons of the dumpling mixture and drop them into the pot. Try to keep them separated and mostly submerged, without disturbing them too much.

5. Reduce Sauté heat to low and cook for 12 to 15 minutes, loosely covered with the top without locking it, until the dumplings have doubled in size.

6. Meanwhile, bone the chicken, remove and discard the skin, and shred the meat. Add back to the pot and serve in bowls.

COOKING TIP: Even though you end up removing the skin, dredging the chicken and browning it first gives the saucy part of this dish more flavor and body.

INSTANT POT TIP: Loosely covering the mixture while the dumplings cook helps steam them through, making sure they're fully cooked and puffy. It's important not to cover too securely or lock the lid in place, as this will lead to a buildup in pressure.

Per Serving Calories: 543; Total Carbohydrates: 40g; Saturated Fat: 14g; Trans Fat: 0g; Fiber: 2g; Protein: 25g; Sodium: 688mg

Mushroom and Chicken Sausage Risotto

GLUTEN-FREE *The pressure cooker is a lifesaver when it comes to this typically labor-intensive dish. Finally you can serve perfectly cooked, creamy risotto to guests without missing the party!*

**PREP: 15 MINUTES • PRESSURE: 6 MINUTES • TOTAL: 30 MINUTES
PRESSURE LEVEL: HIGH • RELEASE: QUICK**

SERVES 5 TO 6

2 tablespoons canola oil

10 to 12 ounces fully cooked chicken sausage, cut into ¼-inch slices

3 tablespoons butter

1 pound mushrooms (cremini, shiitake, oyster, or a mix), thinly sliced

1 medium yellow onion, chopped

3 garlic cloves, minced

3 thyme sprigs, leaves only, plus more leaves for garnish

Kosher salt

Freshly ground black pepper

1 tablespoon soy sauce

½ cup dry white wine or red wine

4 cups good-quality chicken broth, preferably homemade (try the recipe on page 140)

2 cups Arborio or Calrose rice

¼ cup finely grated Parmesan cheese, plus more for serving

1. Select Sauté on high heat. Add the oil.

2. Once hot, add the sausage and cook, stirring, for 5 minutes, until browned. Remove the sausage.

3. Reduce the heat to medium. Melt the butter, then add the mushrooms and onion. Cook, stirring, for 6 minutes until the onion is translucent and the mushrooms are cooked. Add the garlic and cook for 1 minute more. Add the thyme and season with salt and pepper.

4. Add the soy sauce and wine. Cook, scraping up any brown bits off the bottom of the pot, for about 3 minutes, or until the alcohol smell has gone.

5. Add the broth and rice and stir. Secure the lid.

6. Select Manual and cook at high pressure for 6 minutes.

7. Once cooking is complete, use a quick release. Stir. If the risotto is too soupy, select Sauté and cook, uncovered, for a few minutes. Add the Parmesan.

8. Serve topped with Parmesan and a few thyme leaves.

VARIATION TIP: Make this dish vegetarian by simply leaving out the sausage and using vegetable broth.

Per Serving Calories: 415; Total Carbohydrates: 50g; Saturated Fat: 6g; Trans Fat: 0g; Fiber: 2g; Protein: 16g; Sodium: 1030mg

Quick Chicken Tikka Masala

GLUTEN-FREE *Tikka masala is a creamy Indian dish that is full of spice. This version incorporates much of the flavor of the slow-cooked classic, yet has a short cooking time. Served with rice or naan and a salad, it makes a heck of a meal.*

PREP: 10 MINUTES • PRESSURE: 7 MINUTES • TOTAL: 30 MINUTES
PRESSURE LEVEL: HIGH • RELEASE: QUICK

SERVES 4

2 tablespoons butter

1 small onion, chopped

3 garlic cloves, minced

1 (1-inch) piece ginger, peeled and grated

2 teaspoons ground cumin

2 teaspoons paprika

1 teaspoon ground turmeric

Big pinch cayenne

1 tablespoon sugar

1 (14.5-ounce) can diced or crushed tomatoes with juice

4 medium boneless, skinless chicken breasts

½ cup chicken broth

Kosher salt

Freshly ground black pepper

¼ cup heavy cream

Juice of 1 lemon

1. To preheat the Instant Pot, select Sauté on high heat. Add the butter.

2. When the butter sizzles, add the onion, garlic, and ginger and stir. Cook for 3 to 4 minutes, stirring, until the onion is translucent.

3. Select Cancel and add the cumin, paprika, turmeric, and cayenne and stir, scraping the bottom. Add the sugar and tomatoes with juice, stir, then add the chicken and broth. Nestle the chicken in the mixture and season with salt and pepper. Secure the lid.

4. Select Manual and cook on high heat for 7 minutes.

5. Once cooking is complete, use a quick release. Carefully remove the chicken and chop.

6. Select Sauté and simmer for 4 to 5 minutes until the liquid is reduced. While simmering, add the cream and return the chicken to the pot.

7. Add the lemon juice and stir. Season as needed. Serve.

VARIATION TIP: If you're not into spicy food, decrease the amounts of ginger and paprika and exclude the cayenne. If you like heat, add cayenne until your desired level is reached.

Per Serving Calories: 405; Total Carbohydrates: 13g; Saturated Fat: 8g; Trans Fat: 0g; Fiber: 3g; Protein: 43g; Sodium: 521mg

Spiced Coconut Chicken and Rice

GLUTEN-FREE *This punched-up chicken-and-rice dish is inspired by mulligatawny soup, with curry spices, creamy coconut milk, bright ginger, and fresh lime juice.*

PREP: 10 MINUTES • PRESSURE: 17 MINUTES • TOTAL: 45 MINUTES
PRESSURE LEVEL: HIGH • RELEASE: QUICK, NATURAL

SERVES 4 TO 5

1 tablespoon extra-virgin olive oil

1 onion, cut into ¼-inch slices

1 (1-inch) piece ginger, peeled and cut into ¼-inch slices

3 medium garlic cloves, minced

1 tablespoon curry powder

1 teaspoon ground turmeric

2 pounds bone-in, skin-on chicken thighs

Kosher salt

Freshly ground black pepper

1 (14-ounce) can light coconut milk

½ cup water

1⅓ cups jasmine rice, rinsed

2 tablespoons cilantro leaves plus stems, stems and leaves divided

1½ teaspoons sugar

1 lime, halved (one half cut into wedges, for serving)

1. Select Sauté on high heat on the Instant Pot and add the oil.

2. Once hot, add the onion and ginger and sauté for 2 minutes. Add the garlic, curry powder, and turmeric and cook, stirring, for 1 minute.

3. Add the chicken and season with salt and pepper. Add the coconut milk and water. Secure the lid.

4. Select Manual and cook for 13 minutes on high pressure.

5. When cooking is complete, use a quick release. Transfer the chicken to a platter.

6. Add the rice, chopped cilantro stems, and sugar and secure the lid. Select Manual and cook on high pressure for 4 minutes.

7. Meanwhile, remove the skin and bones from the chicken and discard.

8. When the rice is cooked, select Cancel and let naturally release for 10 minutes. Release any remaining steam.

9. Add the chicken back to the pot and add the juice of half the lime. Stir and season with salt and pepper. Serve in bowls topped with cilantro leaves and lime wedges.

VARIATION TIP: To boost the nutritional value, use brown rice, adding an extra ¼ cup water and cooking the rice for 22 minutes on high pressure with a 10-minute natural release.

Per Serving Calories: 835; Total Carbohydrates: 60g; Saturated Fat: 31g; Trans Fat: 0g; Fiber: 7g; Protein: 31g; Sodium: 169mg

"Roasted" Chicken with Tomatoes and Mushrooms

GLUTEN-FREE, PALEO-FRIENDLY *Salty bacon, earthy mushrooms, red wine, and tomatoes make for a juicy chicken dish reminiscent of coq au vin. You can omit the wine, replacing it with chicken broth—but I, for one, wouldn't skip it. Serve with mashed potatoes or polenta.*

PREP: 17 MINUTES • PRESSURE: 10 MINUTES • TOTAL: 35 MINUTES
PRESSURE LEVEL: HIGH • RELEASE: QUICK

SERVES 4

3 bacon slices, cut into ½-inch pieces

1 (3- to 4-pound) chicken, cut into 8 pieces

Kosher salt

Freshly ground black pepper

1 tablespoon extra-virgin olive oil

1 onion, cut into ⅛-inch slices

4 garlic cloves, minced

8 ounces cremini mushrooms, chopped

¾ cup dry red wine

1 (14.5-ounce) can diced or crushed tomatoes with juice

1 bay leaf

1. Select Sauté on high heat on the Instant Pot.

2. Once hot, add the bacon. Cook until lightly crisp, flipping as needed, and drain on a paper towel.

3. Season the chicken with salt and pepper. Turn the heat to high and add the olive oil. Add the chicken, skin-side down, and cook for 5 minutes, or until browned. Transfer to a plate.

4. Add the onion and garlic and cook, stirring, for 2 minutes. Add the mushrooms and cook, stirring, for 3 minutes more.

5. Add the wine and scrape the bottom of the pan to deglaze. Cook for 3 to 5 minutes, until the smell of alcohol is gone. Stir in the tomatoes with juice, bay leaf, and bacon. Return the chicken to the pot, with the dark meat on the bottom and breasts on the top, skin-side up. Secure the lid.

6. Select Manual and cook at high pressure for 10 minutes.

7. Once cooking is complete, use a quick release. Remove the bay leaf and serve.

INSTANT POT TIP: The Poultry setting can be used for this recipe instead of the Manual setting. Adjust the timer to 10 minutes and proceed with the recipe as written.

Per Serving Calories: 738; Total Carbohydrates: 12g; Saturated Fat: 16g; Trans Fat: 0g; Fiber: 3g; Protein: 68g; Sodium: 618mg

Stuffed Turkey Breast

Roasting a whole turkey can be tough to get right, and it makes enough food for a big crowd. If you're feeding fewer than eight people and want to free up your oven for side dishes, try a turkey breast filled with savory bread stuffing instead. If you end up with extra stuffing, put it in a dish and bake it to serve on the side. And you don't have to wait for Thanksgiving to make this dish—it's easy enough to make any time of the year.

PREP: 20 MINUTES • PRESSURE: 25 MINUTES • TOTAL: 1 HOUR, 5 MINUTES • PRESSURE LEVEL: HIGH • RELEASE: NATURAL

SERVES 6 TO 8

5 tablespoons butter, divided

1 large onion, chopped

2 celery stalks, chopped

¾ cup chopped mushrooms

2 garlic cloves, minced

2 tablespoons chopped fresh sage

1 heaping tablespoon chopped fresh parsley

¾ teaspoon kosher salt, plus more for seasoning

¼ teaspoon freshly ground black pepper, plus more for seasoning

2 cups plain breadcrumbs

3 cups chicken broth, divided

1 (2- to 3-pound) boneless, skinless turkey breast, butterflied to an even thickness

1. Preheat the Instant Pot by selecting Sauté.

2. Once hot, add 3 tablespoons of butter. Once the butter is melted, add the onion and celery. Stir and cook for 3 minutes until the onion is translucent. Add the mushrooms and garlic. Stir and cook for 3 minutes more, or until the mushrooms are soft. Select Cancel.

3. Transfer the vegetables and butter to a large bowl. Add the sage, parsley, salt, pepper, and breadcrumbs and mix. Add the broth, a bit at a time, and mix until you get a moist but crumbly texture, using ¾ to 1 cup of broth.

4. Lay the turkey breast top-side down on your work surface. If it isn't an even thickness, pound the thick parts until it's mostly even. Sprinkle with salt and pepper. Spread the stuffing mixture on the breast, making it about as thick as the turkey breast itself, and leaving at least 1 inch on each side. Roll up tightly (but not so tight that the stuffing squeezes out) and secure with kitchen twine. Season the outside of the breast with salt and pepper.

5. Preheat the Instant Pot by selecting Sauté on high heat.

6. Once hot, add the remaining 2 tablespoons of butter. Once melted, brown the stuffed turkey on all sides, about 3 minutes per side. Finish with it lying seam-side down in the pot. Add the remaining 2 cups of chicken broth and secure the lid.

7. Select Manual and cook at high pressure for 25 minutes.

8. Once cooking is complete, use a natural release. This will take 15 to 20 minutes. Remove the turkey and let it rest, tented with foil.

9. Select Sauté on high heat. Reduce the cooking liquid for 10 to 15 minutes until concentrated.

10. Remove the kitchen twine from the turkey and spoon the gravy over the top. Slice and serve.

INGREDIENT TIP: When buying the turkey breast, have the butcher butterfly it for you to save time and effort. Just make sure it fits in your cooker first!

Per Serving Calories: 421; Total Carbohydrates: 37g; Saturated Fat: 7g; Trans Fat: 0g; Fiber: 4g; Protein: 34g; Sodium: 2431mg

One-Pot Penne and Turkey Meatballs

This one-pot meal with lean but satisfying turkey meatballs will please the whole family. The meatballs, pasta, and sauce all cook in the Instant Pot for ease and great flavor. This recipe is generous with meatballs and light on the pasta for a more balanced diet.

PREP: 10 MINUTES • PRESSURE: 5 MINUTES • TOTAL: 25 MINUTES
PRESSURE LEVEL: HIGH • RELEASE: QUICK

SERVES 4

1 pound lean ground turkey

½ cup plain or panko
   breadcrumbs

3 tablespoons grated
   Parmesan cheese, plus
   extra for garnish

¼ yellow onion, finely chopped

2 garlic cloves, minced

1 tablespoon finely chopped
   fresh basil, plus more
   for garnish

1 egg, beaten

½ teaspoon kosher salt

¼ teaspoon freshly ground
   black pepper

3 tablespoons extra-virgin
   olive oil

1 (14.5-ounce) can diced
   tomatoes with juice

1 (14- to 15-ounce) can tomato
   purée or sauce

½ cup water

8 ounces uncooked
   penne pasta

1. In a medium bowl, combine the turkey, breadcrumbs, Parmesan, onion, garlic, basil, egg, salt, and pepper. Mix well.

2. Form 1½-inch meatballs and place on a plate.

3. Preheat the Instant Pot by selecting Sauté on high heat.

4. Once hot, coat the bottom of the pot with the oil. Add the meatballs, one at a time, in close proximity and, if possible, in one layer. Cook for 1 minute.

5. Add the tomatoes with juice, tomato purée or sauce, water, and pasta. Carefully push the pasta down so that it's mostly submerged in the sauce.

6. Select Manual and cook at high pressure for 5 minutes.

7. Once cooking is complete, select Cancel and let it sit for 1 minute. Then use a quick release.

8. Test the pasta. If it isn't cooked enough, select Sauté and simmer on high until the desired texture is reached.

9. Serve topped with more Parmesan and basil.

COOKING TIP: For an extra-quick meal, form your meatballs a few hours in advance and store them in the refrigerator. Pull them out 10 minutes before cook time and proceed with the recipe as written.

Per Serving Calories: 630; Total Carbohydrates: 66g; Saturated Fat: 6g; Trans Fat: 0g; Fiber: 2g; Protein: 35g; Sodium: 1670mg

Duck with Mushrooms and Onions

GLUTEN-FREE, PALEO-FRIENDLY *Duck meat is darker, richer, and juicier than chicken. First, duck legs are seared to create a crispy skin and release some of the excess fat. Then they are cooked until tender with mushrooms, onions, and wine. Make this dish for a date—he or she will definitely be impressed.*

PREP: 10 MINUTES • PRESSURE: 20 MINUTES • TOTAL: 40 MINUTES
PRESSURE LEVEL: HIGH • RELEASE: QUICK

SERVES 4

2 tablespoons canola oil

4 duck legs

Kosher salt

Freshly ground pepper

8 ounces small cipollini or pearl onions

8 ounces sliced mushrooms

4 garlic cloves, minced

½ cup dry red wine

1 cup chicken broth

1. Preheat the Instant Pot by selecting Sauté on high heat. Add the oil.

2. Dry the duck well and season with salt and pepper. Place skin-side down in the pot and cook for about 5 minutes, or until nicely browned. Remove.

3. Turn the heat down to medium. Carefully discard all but 2 tablespoons of the fat and oil in the pot. Add the onions and sauté until lightly browned, about 3 minutes. Add the mushrooms and garlic. Cook, stirring, for 3 minutes more.

4. Add the wine and scrape up any brown bits off the bottom of the pot, cooking for 1 minute. Add the broth and duck. Secure the lid.

5. Select Manual and cook at high pressure for 20 minutes.

6. Once cooking is complete, use a quick release. Serve the duck with the onions and mushrooms and spoon over some of the cooking liquid.

SUBSTITUTION TIP: To make this dish more Paleo-friendly, use avocado oil instead of canola oil.

Per Serving Calories: 269; Total Carbohydrates: 9g; Saturated Fat: 2g; Trans Fat: 0g; Fiber: 2g; Protein: 26g; Sodium: 318mg

BEEF, LAMB, AND PORK

Sunday Pot Roast

GLUTEN-FREE *This crowd-pleasing roast is quick enough to cook on a weeknight. The pressure cooker transforms the meat into a fork-tender roast in record time. Potatoes, parsnips, and carrots are added later to keep them from turning mushy.*

PREP: 20 MINUTES • PRESSURE: 1 HOUR, 10 MINUTES
TOTAL: 2 HOURS • PRESSURE LEVEL: HIGH • RELEASE: QUICK, NATURAL

SERVES 6 TO 8

2 tablespoons canola oil

1 (3-pound) beef chuck roast

Kosher salt

Freshly ground black pepper

1 large onion, halved and sliced

4 garlic cloves, minced

4 fresh thyme sprigs

1 bay leaf

1¾ cups or 1 (14.5-ounce) can beef broth

1 pound new potatoes, halved, no bigger than 1-inch pieces

4 to 5 large carrots, cut into ¾-inch pieces

3 large parsnips, cut into ¾-inch pieces

1. To preheat the Instant Pot, select Sauté on high heat. Add the oil.

2. Season the roast with salt and pepper. Once the pot is hot, brown the roast on all sides, 3 to 4 minutes per side. Transfer the meat to a plate.

3. Add the onion and cook for 3 to 5 minutes until starting to brown. Add the garlic, thyme, bay leaf, and broth. Scrape the bottom of the pot to deglaze the pan. Return the meat to the pot and secure the lid.

4. Select Manual and cook at high pressure for 1 hour.

5. When cooking is complete, use a quick release. Add the potatoes, carrots, and parsnips, submerging them in the cooking liquid.

6. Select Manual and cook at high heat for 10 minutes.

7. When cooking is complete, use a natural release for 10 minutes and then release any remaining steam.

8. The potatoes should be fork-tender and the meat should be falling apart. Serve topped with the juice.

INSTANT POT TIP: The Meat/Stew function can be used for the first part of this recipe. Adjust the function's cook time to 1 hour.

Per Serving Calories: 1011; Total Carbohydrates: 32g; Saturated Fat: 26g; Trans Fat: 0g; Fiber: 7g; Protein: 64g; Sodium: 444mg

Barbecue Beef Brisket

GLUTEN-FREE *This brisket may not be cooked on a barbecue, but it has all of that sweet, tangy, and meaty flavor. It's a great dish for the Jewish holidays or a summer gathering. Serve as is or on hamburger buns.*

PREP: 10 MINUTES • PRESSURE: 1 HOUR, 30 MINUTES
TOTAL: 2 HOURS, 10 MINUTES • PRESSURE LEVEL: HIGH
RELEASE: NATURAL

SERVES 8

3 tablespoons canola oil

1 (4-pound) beef brisket, trimmed of excess fat and quartered

Kosher salt

Freshly ground black pepper

1 large onion, cut into ⅛-inch slices

4 garlic cloves, minced

1 (6-ounce) can tomato sauce

1 cup water

⅓ cup brown sugar

2 tablespoons brown mustard

1 tablespoon Worcestershire sauce

2 teaspoons smoked paprika

1 teaspoon chili powder

3 tablespoons apple cider vinegar

1. Preheat the Instant Pot by selecting Sauté on high heat. Add the oil.

2. Season the brisket with salt and pepper. Once the pot is hot, brown the brisket on all sides, about 3 minutes per side. Remove and set aside.

3. Add the onion and garlic and sauté for 3 minutes. Add the tomato sauce, water, brown sugar, mustard, Worcestershire, paprika, and chili powder and stir. Add the meat and secure the lid.

4. Select Manual and cook at high pressure for 1½ hours.

5. Once cooking is complete, let the pressure release naturally for 10 minutes. Release any remaining pressure.

6. Using tongs, remove the meat and let it rest. Select Sauté on high heat and add the vinegar. Simmer the sauce until thick, 10 to 15 minutes. Slice the meat against the grain and return it to the sauce. Serve.

VARIATION TIP: For a more traditional holiday brisket, leave out the mustard, Worcestershire, paprika, and chili powder.

Per Serving Calories: 514; Total Carbohydrates: 11g; Saturated Fat: 6g; Trans Fat: 0g; Fiber: 1g; Protein: 70g; Sodium: 338mg

One-Pot Pasta Bolognese

Pasta with meat sauce is a dinner favorite, and simplifying things by cooking the sauce and pasta together means it will be a cook's favorite, too. If you don't have ground beef, ground turkey, lamb, or pork will work, too.

PREP: 10 MINUTES • PRESSURE: 5 MINUTES • TOTAL: 30 MINUTES
PRESSURE LEVEL: HIGH • RELEASE: QUICK

SERVES 4

1 tablespoon extra-virgin
   olive oil

12 ounces lean ground beef

1 large onion, chopped

3 garlic cloves, minced

½ cup dry red wine

½ teaspoon kosher salt, plus
   more for seasoning

¼ teaspoon red pepper flakes

1½ cups water

12 ounces uncooked penne
   pasta (with a 9- to 13-minute
   cook time)

1 (28-ounce) can crushed
   tomatoes in purée or good
   tomato sauce

½ cup shredded
   mozzarella cheese

1. Preheat the Instant Pot by selecting Sauté on high heat.

2. Wait 1 minute and then add the oil. Add the ground beef and use a wooden spoon or spatula to break up and stir as it cooks, about 3 minutes.

3. Once the meat is browned and cooked, add the onion and stir. Cook for 1 minute and add the garlic. Cook for 1 minute more.

4. Add the wine and scrape the bottom to deglaze the pan. Cook for 1 to 2 minutes, or until the alcohol smell has gone away.

5. Add the salt, red pepper flakes, and water and stir. Add the pasta and stir. Pour the tomatoes or tomato sauce over in an even layer, covering the pasta. Secure the lid.

6. Select Manual and cook at high pressure for 5 minutes.

7. Once cooking is complete, use a quick release. Test the pasta. If it isn't quite done, select Sauté and simmer for another 1 to 2 minutes. Serve topped with mozzarella.

INGREDIENT TIP: Replace up to half of the water with beef broth for an extra boost of flavor.

Per Serving Calories: 596; Total Carbohydrates: 68g; Saturated Fat: 4g; Trans Fat: 0g; Fiber: 7g; Protein: 45g; Sodium: 841mg

Five-Spice Boneless Beef Ribs

Boneless beef ribs are made unbelievably tender and flavorful in record time thanks to the magic of pressure cooking. Chinese five-spice powder, fresh ginger, soy sauce, and sugar make a salty-sweet, Asian-style sauce. Serve over steamed rice.

PREP: 15 MINUTES • PRESSURE: 35 MINUTES • TOTAL: 1 HOUR, 15 MINUTES • PRESSURE LEVEL: HIGH • RELEASE: NATURAL

SERVES 6

6 boneless beef short ribs, trimmed

2 teaspoons Chinese five-spice powder

Kosher salt

2 tablespoons canola oil

4 garlic cloves, minced

1 (1-inch) piece fresh ginger, peeled and finely chopped

2 tablespoons rice wine vinegar

½ cup beef broth

¼ cup soy sauce

¼ cup raw sugar or brown sugar

1. Preheat the oven to broil.

2. Coat the ribs with the five-spice powder and season with salt. Place on a baking sheet and broil them for 3 minutes on each side.

3. Preheat the Instant Pot by selecting Sauté. Add the oil.

4. Add the garlic and ginger and sauté for 2 minutes, until starting to brown. Add the vinegar and cook for 1 minute. Select Cancel and add the broth, soy sauce, and sugar and stir until the sugar dissolves. Add the ribs and secure the lid.

5. Select Manual and cook at high pressure for 35 minutes.

6. Once cooking is complete, use a natural release. This will take about 15 minutes.

7. Remove the ribs and place them back on the baking sheet. Brush with the cooking liquid and broil again for 3 minutes per side to form a crust.

8. Meanwhile, select Sauté on high heat and reduce the sauce by up to half.

9. After broiling, brush the ribs on all sides with the sauce. Serve with extra sauce.

INGREDIENT TIP: Chinese five-spice powder is a blend of star anise, cloves, Sichuan peppercorns, cinnamon, and fennel. It can be found in the spice aisle or international section of the grocery store or at specialty markets.

Per Serving Calories: 247; Total Carbohydrates: 10g; Saturated Fat: 2g; Trans Fat: 0g; Fiber: 0g; Protein: 27g; Sodium: 746mg

Corned Beef

Corned beef usually takes many hours to cook, but the pressure cooker changes all of that. In just a couple of hours, a piece of tender and flavorful meat will emerge from your cooker ready to eat. Serve with the Horseradish Mashed Potatoes on page 48 and the Braised Cabbage on page 42 for an Irish feast.

PREP: 5 MINUTES • PRESSURE: 1 HOUR, 30 MINUTES
TOTAL: 2 HOURS • PRESSURE LEVEL: HIGH • RELEASE: NATURAL

SERVES 8

1 (3½- to 4-pound) flat-cut
    corned beef

1 (12-ounce) bottle beer
    (lager or pilsner is best)

2 cups chicken broth

1 onion, quartered

1 bay leaf

Freshly ground black pepper

1. Rinse the corned beef and pat dry. Trim off the excess fat, leaving a thin layer.

2. Place the corned beef in the Instant Pot and cover with the beer and broth. Add the onion and bay leaf and season with pepper. Secure the lid.

3. Select Manual and cook at high pressure for 1½ hours.

4. Once cooking is complete, use a natural release. This will take 15 to 20 minutes.

5. Using tongs, remove the meat and let it rest a few minutes before slicing.

INGREDIENT TIP: If you forgot to pick up chicken broth, replace it with water. It will still be flavorful.

Per Serving Calories: 388; Total Carbohydrates: 3g; Saturated Fat: 0g; Trans Fat: 0g; Fiber: 0g; Protein: 28g; Sodium: 1876mg

Oxtail Ragu

GLUTEN-FREE *Tough but flavorful oxtails become so tender after just an hour of pressure cooking that the meat falls apart into the sauce. Serve over a bed of Parmesan polenta or fresh pasta.*

PREP: 20 MINUTES • PRESSURE: 1 HOUR • TOTAL: 1 HOUR, 40 MINUTES • PRESSURE LEVEL: HIGH • RELEASE: NATURAL

SERVES 4

2 tablespoons canola oil

12 (3-inch) oxtail pieces, rinsed and dried

Kosher salt

Freshly ground black pepper

2 tablespoons butter

1 onion, chopped

2 carrots, peeled and chopped

2 celery stalks, chopped

½ cup dry red wine

1 (28-ounce) can whole tomatoes, drained

½ cup beef broth or water

Pinch red pepper flakes

1. Preheat the Instant Pot by selecting Sauté on high heat. Add the oil.

2. Season the oxtails well with salt and pepper. Once the pot is hot, add half of the oxtails in a single layer. Cook for about 4 minutes, or until browned. Flip and repeat on the other side. Repeat with the rest of the oxtails and set aside.

3. Carefully drain all but 1 to 2 tablespoons of the fat.

4. Add the butter. Once melted, add the onion, carrots, and celery. Cook, stirring occasionally, for 2 minutes. Add the wine and scrape up any brown bits off the bottom of the pot. Cook for about 2 minutes, or until the smell of alcohol goes away.

5. Add the tomatoes, crushing them with your hands before dropping them into the pot. Add the broth and red pepper flakes. Season with salt and pepper and secure the lid.

6. Select Manual and cook at high pressure for 1 hour.

7. Once cooking is complete, use a natural release. This will take 15 to 20 minutes.

8. Remove the oxtails and carefully strip the meat off the bones. Add the meat back to the sauce and stir. Serve.

SUBSTITUTION TIP: To make this dish Paleo, use olive oil instead of butter and ¼ cup broth instead of wine.

Per Serving Calories: 621; Total Carbohydrates: 15g; Saturated Fat: 13g; Trans Fat: 0g; Fiber: 4g; Protein: 55g; Sodium: 544mg

Lamb Curry

GLUTEN-FREE *Traditional South Indian lamb curry combines a number of aromatic spices to create layers of flavor without overwhelming the lamb. This recipe is a simpler version of the dish, using garam masala—a blend of several Indian spices—to simulate the flavors. Marinating your lamb is the secret to this dish, so let it sit for at least 30 minutes. Serve with steamed jasmine rice or naan.*

PREP: 5 MINUTES, PLUS AT LEAST 30 MINUTES TO MARINATE
PRESSURE: 20 MINUTES • TOTAL: 1 HOUR, 15 MINUTES
PRESSURE LEVEL: HIGH • RELEASE: NATURAL

SERVES 4 TO 6

1½ pounds boneless lamb, trimmed of fat and cut into 1-inch cubes

Kosher salt

Freshly ground black pepper

1 (1-inch) piece fresh ginger, peeled and grated

4 garlic cloves, minced

⅓ cup plain yogurt

1 tablespoon butter

1 small onion, diced

2½ teaspoons garam masala

½ teaspoon turmeric

1 (14.5-ounce) can diced tomatoes, with juice

Fresh cilantro, for garnish

1. Season the lamb with salt and pepper. In a large bowl, combine the lamb, ginger, garlic, and yogurt. Let marinate for at least 30 minutes or up to 8 hours in the refrigerator.

2. Add the lamb and all of its liquid, along with the butter, onion, garam masala, turmeric, and tomatoes with juice to the Instant Pot. Season with salt and pepper and stir. Secure the lid.

3. Select Manual and cook at high pressure for 20 minutes.

4. Once cooking is complete, use a natural release. If a thicker sauce is desired, select Sauté and cook on high heat until the sauce has thickened.

5. Top with fresh cilantro and serve.

INGREDIENT TIP: Garam masala can typically be found in the spice section or the international aisle of your grocery store.

Per Serving Calories: 391; Total Carbohydrates: 9g; Saturated Fat: 7g; Trans Fat: 0g; Fiber: 2g; Protein: 51g; Sodium: 214mg

Lamb and Feta Meatballs with Tomato and Olive Sauce

Ground lamb is mixed with feta cheese and herbs to form tender, Greek-inspired meatballs in this easy dish. The meatballs and sauce cook simultaneously, making dinner extra fast.

PREP: 10 MINUTES • PRESSURE: 8 MINUTES • TOTAL: 30 MINUTES
PRESSURE LEVEL: HIGH • RELEASE: QUICK

1. In a large bowl, combine the lamb, egg, breadcrumbs, feta, parsley, mint, water, half of the minced garlic, salt, and pepper. Form into 1-inch balls.

2. Preheat the Instant Pot by selecting Sauté.

3. Once hot, add the oil followed by the onion and bell pepper. Cook for 2 minutes and add the remaining minced garlic. Cook for 1 minute more.

4. Stir in the crushed tomatoes with juice, tomato sauce, and oregano. Season with salt and pepper. Add the meatballs and carefully spoon the sauce over them. Secure the lid.

5. Select Manual and cook at high pressure for 8 minutes.

6. Once cooking is complete, use a quick release. Check a meatball to make sure it's cooked through. Serve with the sauce topped with olives (if using), and a sprinkle of feta and parsley.

INSTANT POT TIP: You can use the Stew function for this dish. Adjust the timer to 8 minutes and proceed with the recipe as written.

Per Serving Calories: 384; Total Carbohydrates: 17g; Saturated Fat: 6g; Trans Fat: 0g; Fiber: 3g; Protein: 38g; Sodium: 904mg

SERVES 6 TO 8

1½ pounds ground lamb

1 egg, beaten

½ cup plain breadcrumbs

½ cup crumbled feta cheese, plus extra for garnish

2 tablespoons finely chopped fresh parsley, plus extra for garnish

1 tablespoon finely chopped fresh mint

1 tablespoon water

4 garlic cloves, minced, divided

½ teaspoon kosher salt, plus more for sauce

¼ teaspoon freshly ground black pepper, plus more for sauce

2 tablespoons extra-virgin olive oil

1 medium onion, chopped

1 medium green bell pepper, chopped

1 (28-ounce) can crushed tomatoes with juice

1 (6-ounce) can tomato sauce

1 teaspoon dried oregano

⅓ cup pitted and chopped Kalamata olives (optional)

Baby Back Ribs

Not only can you have succulent baby back ribs in under an hour with a pressure cooker, but it's arguably the best way to cook ribs. It breaks down the tough meat in record time while keeping it juicy and flavorful. Finishing the ribs in the oven gives them a nice sticky coating.

**PREP: 10 MINUTES • PRESSURE: 30 MINUTES • TOTAL: 55 MINUTES
PRESSURE LEVEL: HIGH • RELEASE: QUICK**

SERVES 4

2 tablespoons kosher salt

1 tablespoon brown sugar

1 tablespoon chili powder

1 tablespoon paprika

2 teaspoons garlic powder

1½ teaspoons cayenne

1 teaspoon freshly ground black pepper

1 (3- to 4-pound) rack baby back ribs

1 cup beef broth or water

Barbecue sauce (try the recipe on page 145)

1. In a small bowl, combine the salt, brown sugar, chili powder, paprika, garlic powder, cayenne, and black pepper.

2. Cut the rack of ribs into 4 equal pieces. Rub all sides of each piece with the spice rub.

3. Add the broth to the Instant Pot. Add the ribs to the pot in a teepee formation and secure the lid.

4. Select Manual and cook on high pressure for 30 minutes.

5. Preheat the oven to 425°F. Line a baking sheet with foil.

6. Once cooking is complete, use a quick release.

7. Use tongs to move the ribs to the baking sheet. Brush the ribs on all sides with the barbecue sauce and bake for 7 minutes on each side.

8. Serve as racks or cut into individual ribs.

INGREDIENT TIP: Homemade barbecue sauce is truly delicious, but a bottled version will do in a pinch.

Per Serving Calories: 659; Total Carbohydrates: 21g; Saturated Fat: 2g; Trans Fat: 0g; Fiber: 2g; Protein: 63g; Sodium: 2006mg

Pulled Pork

Making juicy and flavorful pulled pork is typically an all-day affair, but with a pressure cooker, it's ready in less than two hours. Chunks of boneless pork roast, also known as Boston butt, cook until fork-tender in a mix of spices and natural juices, making this recipe largely hands-off. It even produces its own barbecue sauce.

PREP: 5 MINUTES • PRESSURE: 45 MINUTES • TOTAL: 1 HOUR, 30 MINUTES • PRESSURE LEVEL: HIGH • RELEASE: NATURAL

SERVES 6 TO 8

1 (4-pound) boneless pork roast, trimmed of excess fat

3 packed tablespoons brown sugar

2 tablespoons chili powder

2 tablespoons smoked paprika

1 teaspoon ground cumin

1 teaspoon kosher salt

½ teaspoon freshly ground white pepper

¾ cup apple cider or water

½ cup apple cider vinegar

½ cup ketchup

6 to 8 soft hamburger buns

1. Cut the pork roast against the grain into 4 equal pieces.

2. In a small bowl, combine the brown sugar, chili powder, paprika, cumin, salt, and pepper. Rub the pork roast on all sides with the spice mixture.

3. Add the apple cider or water, vinegar, and ketchup to the Instant Pot and stir. Add the spice-rubbed pork and secure the lid.

4. Select Manual and cook at high pressure for 45 minutes.

5. Once cooking is complete, select Cancel and use a natural release. This will take about 15 minutes.

6. Transfer the pork to a plate and let it cool slightly. Shred with a fork, trimming off and discarding any extra fat.

7. Skim excess fat from the cooking liquid. Select Sauté and simmer the sauce for about 20 minutes, or until it measures at the 2-cup line. Season with salt and pepper if needed.

8. Add half of the sauce to the pork and stir to combine. Serve on soft hamburger buns with more sauce.

SUBSTITUTION TIP: Freshly ground black pepper can be used in place of white pepper, if needed.

Per Serving Calories: 624; Total Carbohydrates: 37g; Saturated Fat: 4g; Trans Fat: 0g; Fiber: 3g; Protein: 84g; Sodium: 1019mg

One-Pot Beans, Sausage, and Greens

GLUTEN-FREE *When the weather turns cold and you want a meal that's wholesome and comforting, a steamy pot of tender beans, meaty sausage, and flavorful greens is just what the doctor ordered. Using canned beans makes this an ultra-fast meal—ready in less than 30 minutes.*

PREP: 10 MINUTES • PRESSURE: 5 MINUTES • TOTAL: 25 MINUTES
PRESSURE LEVEL: HIGH • RELEASE: QUICK

SERVES 4 TO 6

1 tablespoon extra-virgin olive oil

12 ounces Italian-style or hot sausage, without casing

1 medium yellow onion, chopped

3 garlic cloves, minced

1 large bunch collard greens, stemmed and chopped

2 (15-ounce) cans pinto beans, rinsed and drained

½ cup chicken broth or water

Kosher salt

Freshly ground black pepper

1. To preheat the Instant Pot, select Sauté.

2. Once hot, add the oil followed by the sausage. Cook, breaking apart with a wooden spoon or spatula, until the sausage is browned and cooked through. Remove the sausage and set aside.

3. Add the onion to the pot and cook for 2 minutes. Add the garlic and cook for 1 minute more, or until the onions are translucent.

4. Add the greens, beans, and broth, and season with salt and pepper. Stir. Secure the lid.

5. Select Manual and cook at high pressure for 5 minutes.

6. Once cooking is complete, select Cancel and use a quick release.

7. Taste and adjust the seasoning. If you want less liquid, select Sauté on high heat and cook for up to 5 minutes.

INGREDIENT TIP: Prepare your collard greens by filling your sink basin with cold water. Separate the leaves and submerge, swishing around. Let them sit for a few minutes and the dirt will sink to the bottom. Drain the leaves and dry them before tearing the leafy greens off the stems in large chunks. Roll the greens into a cigar shape and slice them.

Per Serving Calories: 648; Total Carbohydrates: 60g; Saturated Fat: 9g; Trans Fat: 0g; Fiber: 21g; Protein: 37g; Sodium: 1282mg

Teriyaki Pork Loin

Meaty pork loin roast is marinated in soy sauce, pineapple juice, and ginger for lots of sweet and salty flavor. You can technically skip the marinating step, but it's worth thinking ahead!

PREP: 10 MINUTES, PLUS AT LEAST 2 HOURS TO MARINATE
PRESSURE: 25 MINUTES • TOTAL: 2 HOURS, 50 MINUTES
PRESSURE LEVEL: HIGH • RELEASE: NATURAL

SERVES 4 TO 6

1 (2- to 2½-pound) boneless pork loin roast, trimmed of excess fat

½ cup lower-sodium soy sauce

½ cup pineapple juice

3 tablespoons brown sugar

6 garlic cloves, minced, divided

1 heaping teaspoon grated fresh ginger

2 tablespoons canola oil

1 large red onion, cut into ⅛-inch slices

2 tablespoons rice wine vinegar

1. In a large bowl or large resealable plastic bag, combine the pork, soy sauce, pineapple juice, brown sugar, 2 of the minced garlic cloves, and the grated ginger. Marinate in the refrigerator for at least 2 hours or overnight.

2. Select Sauté on high heat on the Instant Pot and add the oil.

3. Remove the roast from the marinade and let drain, reserving the marinade. Brown the roast in the oil on all sides, about 3 minutes per side. Transfer the meat to a plate.

4. With the pot still on Sauté, add the onion and cook, stirring frequently, for 3 minutes until starting to brown. Add the remaining 4 minced garlic cloves and cook for 1 minute more. Add the roast and the reserved marinade, adding a little water if needed to bring the total liquid to 1 cup. Secure the lid.

5. Select Manual and cook at high pressure for 25 minutes.

6. Once cooking is complete, use a natural release. Test the pork for doneness—it should be at least 140°F in the center. Remove the roast and let it rest. Add the vinegar to the sauce.

7. Select Sauté and simmer for 5 minutes to reduce the sauce.

8. Serve the meat sliced, with sauce spooned over the top.

VARIATION TIP: For even more fruity flavor, toss in 1 cup chopped pineapple.

Per Serving Calories: 485; Total Carbohydrates: 20g; Saturated Fat: 3g; Trans Fat: 0g; Fiber: 1g; Protein: 63g; Sodium: 1146mg

Pork Fried Rice

Make a classic takeout dish in about the same time it would take for the delivery to arrive. Plus, it's healthier and you'll end up with only one pot to wash. Swap the pork for beef if you like.

PREP: 12 MINUTES • PRESSURE: ABOUT 10 MINUTES
TOTAL: 40 MINUTES • PRESSURE LEVEL: LOW • RELEASE: NATURAL

1. Preheat the Instant Pot by selecting Sauté on high heat.

2. Add 1 tablespoon of oil, followed by the onion and carrot. Cook, stirring frequently, for 2 minutes.

3. Season the pork with salt and pepper and add it to the pot. Cook, stirring occasionally, for 5 minutes more, or until the pork is cooked through.

4. Select Cancel and remove the pork, onion, and carrot. Add the water and scrape the bottom of the pan to remove any browned bits. Add the rice and a pinch of salt and secure the lid.

5. Select Rice and cook for the automated amount of time (8 to 15 minutes).

6. Once cooking is complete, select Cancel and let naturally release for 10 minutes. Vent any remaining steam.

7. Stir the rice and push it up against the sides, exposing the bottom of the pot in the middle.

SERVES 4

3 tablespoons canola oil, divided

1 small onion, finely chopped

1 medium carrot, peeled and finely chopped

8 ounces thin pork loin chop, cut into ½-inch pieces

Kosher salt

Freshly ground black pepper

3 cups plus 2 tablespoons water

2 cups long-grain white rice

1 egg, beaten

½ cup frozen peas

3 tablespoons soy sauce

8. Select Sauté. Once hot, add the remaining 2 tablespoons of oil.

9. Add the egg, and scramble it while it cooks.

10. When the egg is mostly cooked, add the peas along with the onion, carrot, and pork. Stir the rice into the mixture and cook, stirring occasionally, for a few minutes.

11. Select Cancel, stir in the soy sauce, and serve immediately.

INSTANT POT TIP: You can swap out the white rice for brown. Consult your Instant Pot manual or the Electric Pressure Cooking Time Charts at the back of this book for the correct cook times.

Per Serving Calories: 547; Total Carbohydrates: 81g; Saturated Fat: 2g; Trans Fat: 0g; Fiber: 3g; Protein: 22g; Sodium: 867mg

Easy Hawaiian-Style Pork ✓

GLUTEN-FREE, PALEO-FRIENDLY *Kālua is a traditional Hawaiian cooking method that utilizes an underground oven and a low and very slow cooking method. It yields super juicy meat, but isn't exactly practical for making at home. In comes the pressure cooker, which simulates hours and hours of slow cooking in less than two hours. Serve with braised cabbage, rice, or grilled pineapple and peppers.*

PREP: 5 MINUTES • PRESSURE: 1 HOUR, 30 MINUTES
TOTAL: 2 HOURS • PRESSURE LEVEL: HIGH • RELEASE: NATURAL

1. Cut the pork roast into 3 equal pieces. Place in the bottom of the Instant Pot in a single layer.

2. Add the onion, garlic, and salt, and season with pepper. Add the water and secure the lid.

3. Select Manual and cook at high pressure for 1½ hours.

4. Once cooking is complete, select Cancel and use a natural pressure release. This will take 15 to 20 minutes.

5. Shred the pork and serve with the juice.

INGREDIENT TIP: You can find Hawaiian salt in specialty and health food stores or order it online. Smoked sea salt will work in a pinch.

Per Serving Calories: 536; Total Carbohydrates: 2g; Saturated Fat: 13g; Trans Fat: 0g; Fiber: 0g; Protein: 51g; Sodium: 3509mg

SERVES 8

1 (5-pound) bone-in pork roast

1 onion, quartered

6 garlic cloves, minced

1½ tablespoons red Hawaiian coarse salt or 1 tablespoon red Hawaiian fine salt

Freshly ground black pepper

1 cup water

Great! Has great flavor. We served w/ BBQ sauce.

German Sausages with Peppers and Onions

Beer-braised bratwursts are a popular German dish, especially during Oktoberfest. Cooking the sausages in the pressure cooker locks in the flavor and juices and makes the dish an easy weeknight meal. If you're feeding more than four, add more sausages and veggies as needed and ⅓ cup beer per sausage.

**PREP: 12 MINUTES • PRESSURE: 10 MINUTES • TOTAL: 40 MINUTES
PRESSURE LEVEL: HIGH • RELEASE: NATURAL**

SERVES 4

2 tablespoons butter or canola oil

4 large German sausages, such as bratwurst

1 large onion, halved and cut into ¼-inch slices

1 green bell pepper, seeded and cut into ¼-inch rings

1 red bell pepper, seeded and cut into ¼-inch rings

1 (12-ounce) bottle German-style lager

Kosher salt

Freshly ground black pepper

4 hoagie rolls

Good-quality mustard, for serving

1. To preheat the Instant Pot, select Sauté. Add the butter or oil.

2. Once hot, add the sausages. Brown them on both sides. This will take 5 to 10 minutes.

3. Remove the sausages and turn the heat to high. Add the onion and stir. Cook for 4 to 5 minutes until the onion starts to brown.

4. Add the peppers and lager and stir. Cook for 1 minute. Season with salt and pepper. Add the sausages and secure the lid.

5. Select Manual and cook at high pressure for 10 minutes.

6. Once cooking is complete, use a natural release. Serve the sausages on hoagie rolls topped with the peppers and onions and mustard.

SUBSTITUTION TIP: If you don't want to use beer, replace it with beef broth. You can also use nonalcoholic beer, although the sausages and veggies don't really absorb any alcohol.

Per Serving Calories: 624; Total Carbohydrates: 57g; Saturated Fat: 13g; Trans Fat: 0g; Fiber: 9g; Protein: 23g; Sodium: 1266mg

CHAPTER EIGHT

DESSERT

Carrot Cake Rice Pudding

VEGETARIAN, GLUTEN-FREE *Creamy rice pudding is just a few minutes away! This version has all of the major components of carrot cake—brown sugar, coconut, raisins, shredded carrots—without the hassle of baking a cake. Using a natural release will ensure good texture and prevent the pudding from splattering.*

PREP: 10 MINUTES • PRESSURE: 12 MINUTES • TOTAL: 35 MINUTES
PRESSURE LEVEL: HIGH • RELEASE: NATURAL

SERVES 5 TO 6

1 cup Arborio rice

1 (14-ounce) can coconut milk

2 cups milk

½ cup finely shredded carrot

¼ teaspoon table salt

¼ cup packed brown sugar

1 large egg, well beaten

1 teaspoon vanilla extract

½ cup sweetened shredded coconut

⅓ cup raisins

½ teaspoon ground cinnamon

¼ teaspoon ground ginger

1. Add the rice, coconut milk, milk, carrot, and salt to the pressure cooker and stir. Secure the lid.

2. Select Manual and cook at high pressure for 12 minutes.

3. Once cooking is complete, use a natural release. This will take about 10 minutes.

4. Select Sauté and add the brown sugar, egg, and vanilla and stir well. Once the mixture begins to boil, select Cancel. Add the coconut, raisins, cinnamon, and ginger.

5. Let cool for a few minutes, as the pudding will thicken as it sits. Serve warm or cold.

SUBSTITUTION TIP: If you don't have coconut milk, increase the quantity of milk to 3½ cups. To make the recipe nondairy, replace the milk with water.

Per Serving Calories: 647; Total Carbohydrates: 82g; Saturated Fat: 27g; Trans Fat: 0g; Fiber: 6g; Protein: 12g; Sodium: 265mg

Molten Brownie Pudding

VEGETARIAN *Totally decadent, this ultra-chocolaty dessert is not for the faint of heart. Once cooked, the pudding is creamy, buttery, and rich, with all of the flavors of a good brownie. Serve with a scoop of vanilla ice cream.*

PREP: 15 MINUTES • PRESSURE: 30 MINUTES • TOTAL: 1 HOUR
PRESSURE LEVEL: HIGH • RELEASE: QUICK

SERVES 3 TO 4

1½ cups water

7 tablespoons butter, melted, divided

1 cup sugar

2 eggs

¼ cup all-purpose flour

¼ cup plus 2 tablespoons unsweetened cocoa powder

Pinch table salt

½ teaspoon vanilla

¼ cup semisweet chocolate chips

1. Prepare the Instant Pot by adding the water to the pot and placing the steam rack on top.

2. Butter a 6- to 7-inch soufflé or baking dish with 1 tablespoon of butter. (If your dish doesn't have handles, make a sling with a piece of foil, folded in half twice, that's long enough to go under the dish and stick up 6 inches on each side, creating "handles.")

3. In a large bowl, use an electric mixer to beat together the sugar and eggs until light yellow and fluffy, 3 to 5 minutes.

4. In a small bowl, combine the flour, cocoa powder, and salt and whisk until no lumps remain. Add to the sugar and egg mixture and mix just until combined. Add the vanilla and the remaining 6 tablespoons of melted butter and mix just until combined.

5. Pour the mixture into the prepared baking dish. Top with the chocolate chips and place on the steam rack. Secure the lid.

6. Select Manual and cook at high pressure for 30 minutes. Once cooking is complete, use a quick release. Carefully remove the top so that any condensation doesn't drip on the pudding, then carefully remove the pan using oven mitts or tongs.

7. Let it cool for at least 5 minutes before serving.

Per Serving Calories: 680; Total Carbohydrates: 92g; Saturated Fat: 20g; Trans Fat: 0g; Fiber: 4g; Protein: 8g; Sodium: 346mg

Little Pumpkin Puddings

VEGETARIAN, GLUTEN-FREE *I crave pumpkin pie throughout the fall and winter, but rarely bother to actually bake one. Luckily, these easy-as-pie puddings came along. They're so much quicker to whip up and cook than a whole pie and satisfy all of those pumpkin cravings. These puddings also make a lovely gluten-free Thanksgiving dessert.*

PREP: 5 MINUTES • PRESSURE: 15 MINUTES
TOTAL: 35 MINUTES, PLUS 1 TO 2 HOURS TO COOL
PRESSURE LEVEL: HIGH • RELEASE: NATURAL

SERVES 4

1 cup water

1 tablespoon butter

1 cup pumpkin purée
   (not pumpkin pie filling)

¼ cup sugar

½ teaspoon ground cinnamon

¼ teaspoon table salt

¼ teaspoon ground ginger

Pinch ground cloves

¾ cup half-and-half

1 egg, beaten

1 egg yolk

½ teaspoon vanilla extract

1. Prepare the Instant Pot by adding the water to the pot and placing the steam rack on top.

2. Butter 4 mugs or other 1-cup, heat-proof containers.

3. In a medium bowl, whisk together the pumpkin, sugar, cinnamon, salt, ginger, and cloves until combined. Add the half-and-half, egg, egg yolk, and vanilla and whisk until creamy.

4. Pour the mixture into the containers, dividing evenly, and place side by side on the steam rack. Secure the lid.

5. Select Manual and cook at high pressure for 15 minutes.

6. Once cooking is complete, use a natural release. Carefully remove the lid so that water doesn't drip on the top of the puddings. Let the puddings sit until the steam dies down and then very carefully lift them out.

7. Let cool to room temperature before serving, 1 to 2 hours.

COOKING TIP: Any 1-cup-size heat-proof containers will do, including mugs, baking cups, small soufflé dishes, or ramekins.

Per Serving Calories: 174; Total Carbohydrates: 18g; Saturated Fat: 6g; Trans Fat: 0g; Fiber: 1g; Protein: 4g; Sodium: 205mg

Chocolate and Orange Bread Pudding

VEGETARIAN *Bread pudding cooks happily in the pressure cooker with the steam making it extra fluffy. Orange zest, dark chocolate, and almond extract add rich, sophisticated flavors. It's also a fun way to use up any stale bread you have lying around.*

PREP: 10 MINUTES • PRESSURE: 15 MINUTES • TOTAL: 40 MINUTES
PRESSURE LEVEL: HIGH • RELEASE: NATURAL

SERVES 4 TO 5

2 cups water

1 teaspoon butter

3 large eggs

⅓ cup plus 1 tablespoon sugar, divided

½ cup whole or 2 percent milk

¾ cup heavy cream or half-and-half

2 tablespoons freshly squeezed orange juice

Zest of 1 orange

1 teaspoon almond extract

Pinch table salt

3½ cups stale French bread, cut into ¾-inch cubes

3 ounces high-quality dark or semisweet chocolate, cut into small pieces

1. Prepare the Instant Pot by adding the water to the pot and placing a steam rack on top.

2. Butter a 6- to 7-inch soufflé or baking dish.

3. In a large bowl, whisk together the eggs and ⅓ cup of sugar until well mixed. Add the milk, cream, orange juice, zest, almond extract, and salt. Mix well.

4. Add the bread and toss until all of the bread is coated. Let it sit for 5 minutes, stirring once or twice.

5. Add the chocolate and mix. Pour into the baking dish and press down if needed. Sprinkle the top with the remaining 1 tablespoon of sugar. Place the dish on the steam rack and secure the lid.

6. Select Manual and cook at high pressure for 15 minutes.

7. Once cooking is complete, use a natural release. Be sure to remove the lid carefully and quickly so that condensation doesn't drip on the pudding. Carefully remove the pan using oven mitts or tongs. Serve warm.

VARIATION TIP: If you're making dessert for two, you can easily halve this recipe and cook it in two small ramekins.

COOKING TIP: If your dish doesn't have handles, create a sling with a piece of foil, folded twice, that's long enough to go under the dish and stick up 6 inches on each side, creating "handles."

Per Serving Calories: 467; Total Carbohydrates: 51g; Saturated Fat: 14g; Trans Fat: 0g; Fiber: 1g; Protein: 12g; Sodium: 336mg

Key Lime Cheesecake

VEGETARIAN *The pressure cooker makes phenomenal cheesecake, cooking it equally all the way through so that it's creamy throughout. You'll need a 7-inch springform pan for this recipe, but it's worth the investment. When you taste how good this dessert is, you'll be making cheesecakes left and right.*

PREP: 15 MINUTES • PRESSURE: 15 MINUTES • TOTAL: 40 MINUTES
PRESSURE LEVEL: HIGH • RELEASE: NATURAL

SERVES 6

1½ cups water

3 tablespoons butter, melted, divided

½ cup graham cracker or gingersnap crumbs

1 pound cream cheese

½ cup sugar

2 eggs

2 tablespoons Key lime juice

1 teaspoon Key lime zest

½ teaspoon vanilla extract

1½ tablespoons all-purpose flour

1. Prepare the Instant Pot by adding the water to the pot and placing a steam rack on top.

2. Butter a 7-inch springform pan with 1 tablespoon of butter. (If your pan doesn't have handles, make a sling for it before putting it into the pot. See the Cooking Tip for instructions.)

3. In a small bowl, combine the graham cracker or gingersnap crumbs and remaining 2 tablespoons of butter. Press into the bottom of the pan and almost halfway up the sides.

4. In a large bowl or stand mixer, beat together the cream cheese and sugar until very smooth. Add the eggs and beat until creamy. Add the lime juice, zest, and vanilla and beat until combined. Add the flour and beat just until combined.

5. Pour the mixture into the pan on top of the prepared crust. Place the pan on the steam rack and secure the lid.

6. Select Manual and cook at high pressure for 15 minutes.

7. Once cooking is complete, use a natural release. Carefully remove the lid so that condensation doesn't drip on the top of the cheesecake. Lift out using the handles or foil sling.

8. Let it cool to room temperature and then cover and refrigerate overnight before serving.

VARIATION TIP: Swap out the lime for lemon, or try chocolate cookies for the crust.

COOKING TIP: A 6- or 7-inch baking pan or soufflé dish will come in handy when making a variety of dishes in your Instant Pot. If your dish or steam rack doesn't have handles, create a sling with a piece of foil, folded in half twice, that's long enough to go under the dish and stick up 6 inches on each side, creating "handles."

Per Serving Calories: 444; Total Carbohydrates: 28g; Saturated Fat: 21g; Trans Fat: 0g; Fiber: 1g; Protein: 8g; Sodium: 348mg

Peach and Blueberry Cobbler

VEGETARIAN *Also known as a grunt or slump, this steamed fruit cobbler is easier than most dough-y desserts and ready in record time. The syrupy, almost jammy fruit is crowned with fluffy and tender dumplings that are lightly sweet. Top the warm cobbler with freshly whipped cream or vanilla ice cream.*

PREP: 10 MINUTES • PRESSURE: 10 MINUTES • TOTAL: 35 MINUTES
PRESSURE LEVEL: HIGH • RELEASE: NATURAL

SERVES 4 TO 6

1 cup all-purpose flour

⅓ cup plus 1 tablespoon sugar, divided

1½ teaspoons baking powder

½ teaspoon table salt

¼ teaspoon baking soda

2 tablespoons cold butter, cubed

⅓ cup buttermilk or whole milk

2 cups peeled, sliced frozen peaches

2 cups frozen blueberries

⅓ cup water

1 tablespoon cornstarch

1 teaspoon freshly squeezed lemon or lime juice

Pinch ground nutmeg

1. In a medium bowl, mix together the flour, 1 tablespoon of sugar, the baking powder, salt, and baking soda until well combined. Add the butter and, using your hands, work it into the flour mixture until it resembles a coarse meal. Add the buttermilk or milk and mix just until moistened. Quickly form a shaggy ball of dough and set aside.

2. Select Sauté and add the peaches, blueberries, water, remaining ⅓ cup of sugar, cornstarch, lemon or lime juice, and nutmeg to the Instant Pot. Stir.

3. Cook for 2 or 3 minutes, or until fruit is defrosted and releases some juice. Select Cancel.

4. Tear off 1-inch balls of the dough and nestle on top of the fruit, evenly spaced in one layer (you should have 8 dumplings). Secure the lid.

5. Select Manual and cook at high pressure for 10 minutes.

6. Once cooking is complete, use a natural release. Let it cool for a few minutes, since the liquid will thicken as it sits. Serve warm.

VARIATION TIP: Replace the blueberries with blackberries or raspberries, depending on your taste and what's available. Taste your fruit before adding it to see how sweet it is, in case you need to add more sugar.

Per Serving Calories: 330; Total Carbohydrates: 66g; Saturated Fat: 4g; Trans Fat: 0g; Fiber: 3g; Protein: 5g; Sodium: 438mg

Easy Apple Dumplings

VEGETARIAN *These apple dumplings are super easy thanks to a can of crescent rolls. Each wedge of tart apple gets wrapped in dough and cooks in a mixture of butter, brown sugar, cinnamon, and apple cider. It's a dessert that tastes like fall, but is simple enough to be enjoyed all year long.*

PREP: 10 MINUTES • PRESSURE: 10 MINUTES • TOTAL: 30 MINUTES
PRESSURE LEVEL: HIGH • RELEASE: NATURAL

SERVES 6 TO 8

1 (8-ounce) can crescent rolls

1 large Granny Smith apple, cored, peeled, and cut into 8 large wedges

4 tablespoons butter

½ cup brown sugar

½ teaspoon vanilla extract

1 teaspoon ground cinnamon

Pinch ground nutmeg

¾ cup apple cider

1. Preheat the Instant Pot by selecting Sauté.

2. Open the can of crescent rolls and roll the dough out flat. Roll each wedge of apple in 1 crescent roll.

3. Add the butter to the Instant Pot and select Cancel. Add the sugar, vanilla, cinnamon, and nutmeg and stir until melted.

4. Place the dumplings side by side in the Instant Pot. Drizzle the apple cider along the edges. Secure the lid.

5. Select Manual and cook at high pressure for 10 minutes.

6. Once cooking is complete, use a natural release. Let it cool for a few minutes and serve warm, drizzled with the sugar and cider syrup.

INGREDIENT TIP: Granny Smiths work best since they're nice and tart. If you're using another type of apple, you may want to decrease the sugar a bit.

Per Serving Calories: 267; Total Carbohydrates: 41g; Saturated Fat: 5g; Trans Fat: 0g; Fiber: 2g; Protein: 4g; Sodium: 262mg

White Wine–Poached Pears with Vanilla

VEGETARIAN, GLUTEN-FREE *Poached pears are an easy but impressive dessert that you can prepare up to two days ahead of time. This recipe uses lighter and fruitier white wine along with a vanilla bean and spices to flavor the pears. Serve warm, cold, or at room temperature, with a scoop of vanilla ice cream.*

PREP: 7 MINUTES • PRESSURE: 8 MINUTES • TOTAL: 30 MINUTES
PRESSURE LEVEL: HIGH • RELEASE: NATURAL

SERVES 4

1 bottle white wine

1½ cups sugar

6 firm but ripe pears, peeled

1 cinnamon stick, broken in half

2 whole cloves

1 large vanilla bean pod, split open lengthwise

½ lemon, cut into rounds

1. Add the wine and sugar to the Instant Pot and stir until dissolved. Add the pears, cinnamon stick, cloves, vanilla bean pod, and lemon. Secure the lid.

2. Select Manual and cook at high pressure for 8 minutes.

3. Once cooking is complete, use a natural release. For best results, store the pears in their cooking liquid overnight before proceeding.

4. Remove the pears and set aside. Remove the spices and all but 2 cups of liquid. Select Sauté and cook the sauce until reduced by half, or 5 to 10 minutes.

5. Serve the pears drizzled with the sauce.

VARIATION TIP: Poached pears are often cooked in red wine, so switch out the wine if you like. You may want to add another ½ cup of sugar.

Per Serving Calories: 310; Total Carbohydrates: 74g; Saturated Fat: 0g; Trans Fat: 0g; Fiber: 10g; Protein: 1g; Sodium: 6mg

Sea Salt Dulce de Leche

VEGETARIAN, GLUTEN-FREE *Dulce de leche is a thick, rich, and sweet sauce that's delicious poured over ice cream or pound cake, sandwiched between shortbread cookies, or used in baked goods. A touch of sea salt and vanilla take the flavor over the top, and it's extra easy to make in the pressure cooker. Note that the can must sit overnight before opening, so incorporate eight hours or more of cool-down time into your schedule.*

FAMILY-FRIENDLY

PREP: 5 MINUTES • PRESSURE: 20 MINUTES • TOTAL: 40 MINUTES, PLUS 8 HOURS TO COOL • PRESSURE LEVEL: HIGH • RELEASE: NATURAL

MAKES ALMOST 2 CUPS

1 (14- or 15-ounce) can
    sweetened condensed milk
½ teaspoon vanilla extract
½ teaspoon sea salt, or more
    to taste

1. Remove the label from the sweetened condensed milk. Do not open.

2. Place the steam rack in the Instant Pot. Place the can of sweetened condensed milk on the steam rack without it touching the sides of the pot. Add enough water so that the can is completely submerged. Secure the lid.

3. Select Manual at high pressure and cook for 20 minutes.

4. Once cooking is complete, use a natural release. This will take at least 10 minutes. Turn the Instant Pot off and carefully remove the lid. Do not disturb the can or water. Leave it overnight to cool.

5. Once completely cool, open the can and add the milk to a small bowl. Add the vanilla and salt and mix. For an even creamier texture, whip for a few minutes with an electric mixer in a medium bowl.

COOKING TIP: Since the can is under pressure after cooking, be careful not to jostle the Instant Pot or the can itself after cooking, and do not open the can until it has cooled completely.

Per Serving (¼ cup) Calories: 171; Total Carbohydrates: 29g; Saturated Fat: 3g; Trans Fat: 0g; Fiber: 0g; Protein: 4g; Sodium: 165mg

STOCKS AND SAUCES

≋≋≋≋≋≋≋≋≋≋≋≋≋≋≋≋≋

Homemade Chicken Stock

GLUTEN-FREE, PALEO-FRIENDLY *Homemade chicken stock can be the difference between a good dish and a great dish. It adds layers of flavor to any soup or stew, and it couldn't be easier to make in the Instant Pot. Whip up a big batch—it freezes well.*

PREP: 5 MINUTES • PRESSURE: 1 HOUR • TOTAL: 1 HOUR, 30 MINUTES
PRESSURE LEVEL: HIGH • RELEASE: NATURAL

MAKES 8 CUPS

2 pounds chicken bones
  and parts

1 yellow onion, quartered

1 large garlic clove, smashed

1 carrot, cut into large chunks

1 bay leaf

½ teaspoon kosher salt
  (optional)

1 teaspoon whole black
  peppercorns (optional)

8 cups water

1. Add the chicken, onion, garlic, carrot, bay leaf, salt (if using), and peppercorns (if using) to the pot. Pour the water over. Secure the lid.

2. Select Soup and cook at high pressure for 1 hour.

3. Once cooking is complete, use a natural release. This will take at least 15 minutes.

4. Carefully strain the broth through a fine-mesh strainer or cheesecloth. If you would like to remove the fat, let the stock cool in the refrigerator and remove the fat on top.

5. Store the stock in the refrigerator for a few days or freeze for up to 3 months.

INGREDIENT TIP: For the chicken, leftover meat (raw or cooked), bones, and organs can be used. Whenever you have leftover chicken bones, toss them into a resealable freezer bag and add to it until you have enough to make stock. No need to defrost—just toss in the pot and proceed with the recipe.

Per Serving (1 cup) Calories: 104; Total Carbohydrates: 8g;
Saturated Fat: 1g; Trans Fat: 0g; Fiber: 0g; Protein: 6g; Sodium: 245mg

Vegetable Stock

VEGETARIAN, GLUTEN-FREE, PALEO-FRIENDLY *Vegetable stock is handy to have around for lots of dishes made in the pressure cooker, adding so much more flavor than plain old water. It's also a great way to use up leftover veggies. Use this recipe as a guide, but mix it up depending upon what you have lying around.*

**PREP: 5 MINUTES • PRESSURE: 1 HOUR • TOTAL: 1 HOUR, 30 MINUTES
PRESSURE LEVEL: HIGH • RELEASE: NATURAL**

1. Add the onions, celery, carrots, mushrooms, garlic, parsley, bay leaf, and water to the Instant Pot. Secure the lid.

2. Select Soup and cook at high pressure for 1 hour.

3. Once cooking is complete, use a natural release. This will take at least 15 minutes.

4. Carefully strain the stock using a fine-mesh strainer or cheesecloth. Season with salt (if using).

5. Store the stock in the refrigerator for a few days or freeze for up to 3 months.

VARIATION TIP: Everything's optional but the onion, celery, carrots, and water. Add whatever you have around, like leeks, scallions, other herbs, tomatoes, parsnips, and more.

Per Serving (1 cup) Calories: 42; Total Carbohydrates: 4g; Saturated Fat: 0g; Trans Fat: 0g; Fiber: g; Protein: 0g; Sodium: 120mg

MAKES 8 CUPS

2 onions, quartered

2 celery stalks, quartered

2 carrots, cut into large chunks

10 button mushrooms

4 garlic cloves, smashed

1 small bunch fresh parsley

1 bay leaf

8 cups water

Kosher salt (optional)

Beef Bone Broth

GLUTEN-FREE, PALEO-FRIENDLY *In the cold winter months, nothing is as warming and nourishing as a cup of hot beef bone broth. Making savory broth is arguably one of the pressure cooker's best uses, infusing big flavor in just an hour or two. Roasting the bones is optional, but adds even more flavor and a deeper color.*

PREP: 5 MINUTES, PLUS 30 MINUTES TO ROAST
PRESSURE: 1 HOUR, 30 MINUTES • TOTAL: 2 HOURS, 30 MINUTES
PRESSURE LEVEL: HIGH • RELEASE: NATURAL

MAKES 8 CUPS

2½ pounds beef bones, including short ribs, knuckles, oxtails, and more

1 teaspoon extra-virgin olive oil

1 yellow onion, quartered

2 celery stalks, quartered

1 carrot, cut into large chunks

1 bay leaf

2 teaspoons apple cider vinegar

1 tablespoon fish sauce (optional)

8 cups water

1. Preheat the oven to 400°F.

2. Toss the bones with the oil on a baking sheet and roast for 30 minutes.

3. Once cool enough to handle, add the bones, onion, celery, carrot, bay leaf, vinegar, fish sauce (if using), and water to the Instant Pot. Secure the lid.

4. Select Manual and cook at high pressure for 1½ hours.

5. Once cooking is complete, use a natural release. This will take at least 15 minutes.

6. Skim any fat off the top of the stock, if desired. Carefully strain the broth using a fine-mesh strainer or cheesecloth.

7. Store the broth in the refrigerator for a few days or freeze for up to 3 months.

VARIATION TIP: You can use a mix of different bones (chicken, beef, and pork) if that's what you have on hand.

Per Serving (1 cup) Calories: 54; Total Carbohydrates: 3g; Saturated Fat: 0g; Trans Fat: 0g; Fiber: 0g; Protein: 5g; Sodium: 278mg

Spicy Chicken Bone Broth

GLUTEN-FREE, PALEO-FRIENDLY *A warmly spicy and nourishing chicken broth like this one will warm you down to your bones. Chicken feet help make the broth more gelatinous, but aren't required. The broth can be enjoyed on its own or combined with shredded chicken and noodles for a quick soup.*

PREP: 5 MINUTES • PRESSURE: 1 HOUR, 30 MINUTES
TOTAL: 2 HOURS, 10 MINUTES • PRESSURE LEVEL: HIGH
RELEASE: NATURAL

MAKES 8 CUPS

2½ pounds mixed chicken bones and feet

1 yellow onion, quartered

1 celery stalk, quartered

1 carrot, cut into large chunks

1 (1½-inch) piece ginger, peeled and cut into ¼-inch slices

1 teaspoon whole black peppercorns

1 tablespoon fish sauce

1 teaspoon apple cider vinegar

8 cups water

1. Add the bones, onion, celery, carrot, ginger, peppercorns, fish sauce, vinegar, and water to the Instant Pot. Secure the lid.

2. Select Manual and cook at high pressure for 1½ hours.

3. Once cooking is complete, use a natural release. This will take at least 15 minutes.

4. Skim any fat off the top of the stock, if desired. Carefully strain the broth using a fine-mesh strainer or cheesecloth.

5. Store the broth in the refrigerator for a few days or freeze for up to 3 months.

INGREDIENT TIP: If you don't have leftover bones, pay a visit to your butcher. Make sure you ask for the feet!

Per Serving (1 cup) Calories: 92; Total Carbohydrates: 8g; Saturated Fat: 1g; Trans Fat: 0g; Fiber: 0g; Protein: 6g; Sodium: 356mg

Homemade Ketchup

GLUTEN-FREE *You don't know what you're missing by using store-bought ketchup until you taste the homemade stuff. It's a whole different thing, with more sweet, tart, and salty flavor than its bottled brethren. Give a jar away as a fun gift or store it in the freezer for your next grill-out.*

PREP: 10 MINUTES • PRESSURE: 15 MINUTES • TOTAL: 50 MINUTES
PRESSURE LEVEL: HIGH • RELEASE: NATURAL

MAKES ABOUT 2½ CUPS

2 tablespoons extra-virgin olive oil

1 medium onion, finely chopped

4 garlic cloves, smashed

1 (28-ounce) can whole tomatoes with juice

½ cup red wine vinegar

1 tablespoon tomato paste

1 teaspoon Worcestershire sauce

⅓ cup packed brown sugar

½ teaspoon paprika

¼ teaspoon white pepper

⅛ teaspoon ground allspice

Pinch kosher salt

1. Preheat the Instant Pot by selecting Sauté.

2. Once hot, add the oil followed by the onion. Cook for 3 minutes until the onion is starting to turn translucent. Add the garlic and sauté 1 minute more.

3. Add the tomatoes with juice, crushing the tomatoes with your hand as you add them. Add the vinegar, tomato paste, Worcestershire sauce, brown sugar, paprika, white pepper, and allspice and bring to a simmer. Add a pinch of salt and secure the lid.

4. Select Manual and cook at high pressure for 15 minutes.

5. Once cooking is complete, use a natural release for 10 minutes, then release any remaining pressure.

6. Remove the lid and stir. Taste for seasoning. Select Sauté and cook, stirring occasionally, until reduced and thick, 15 to 20 minutes. Use an immersion blender to blend until smooth, or blend in a food processor.

7. Let it cool and store it in the refrigerator for up to 1 month or the freezer for several months.

VARIATION TIP: Play with the spices in this recipe to make it your own. Add liquid smoke for a smoky flavor or cayenne for a spicy kick.

Per Serving (2 tablespoons) Calories: 36; Total Carbohydrates: 5g; Saturated Fat: 0g; Trans Fat: 0g; Fiber: 1g; Protein: 1g; Sodium: 87mg

Sweet and Tangy Barbecue Sauce

VEGETARIAN, GLUTEN-FREE *For ribs, chicken, and pork chops that are finger-licking good, a great barbecue sauce is key. Making your own is easy, and it's far and away better than the mass-produced sauce at the grocery store. Letting it cool and sit in the refrigerator for a day or two will produce an even more flavorful sauce, so make it up to a week ahead.*

PREP: 10 MINUTES • PRESSURE: 15 MINUTES • TOTAL: 45 MINUTES
PRESSURE LEVEL: HIGH • RELEASE: NATURAL

MAKES ABOUT 2½ CUPS

4 tablespoons butter

1 small onion, finely chopped

3 garlic cloves, minced

1 cup tomato sauce

½ cup ketchup

½ cup apple cider vinegar

½ cup brown sugar

3 tablespoons molasses

1 tablespoon Dijon mustard

1 teaspoon liquid smoke (optional)

¼ teaspoon cayenne

¼ teaspoon freshly ground black pepper

1. Preheat the Instant Pot by selecting Sauté.

2. Once hot, add the butter and let it melt. Add the onion and cook for 3 minutes until it is starting to turn translucent. Add the garlic and sauté 1 minute more.

3. Add the tomato sauce, ketchup, vinegar, brown sugar, molasses, mustard, liquid smoke (if using), cayenne, and pepper. Secure the lid.

4. Select Manual and cook at high pressure for 15 minutes.

5. Once cooking is complete, use a natural release for 10 minutes, then release any remaining pressure.

6. Stir and taste for seasoning. If a thicker sauce is desired, select Sauté and cook, stirring occasionally, for 10 to 15 minutes.

7. Let it cool and store it in the refrigerator for up to 2 weeks or the freezer for several months.

INGREDIENT TIP: Liquid smoke adds a touch of smokiness that works wonders in a barbecue sauce like this one. It's typically found in the supermarket spice aisle, and can also be found online.

Per Serving (2 tablespoons) Calories: 56; Total Carbohydrates: 9g; Saturated Fat: 2g; Trans Fat: 0g; Fiber: 0g; Protein: 0g; Sodium: 159mg

Classic Marinara Sauce

VEGETARIAN, GLUTEN-FREE, PALEO-FRIENDLY *Marinara is in a huge number of Italian and Italian-inspired dishes, so it pays to have a good recipe handy. Most traditional recipes call for an hour or more of simmering on the stove, but this sauce only cooks for 30 minutes. Use it on pasta, pizza, and more.*

PREP: 10 MINUTES • PRESSURE: 30 MINUTES • TOTAL: 50 MINUTES
PRESSURE LEVEL: HIGH • RELEASE: NATURAL

MAKES ABOUT 4 CUPS

2 tablespoons extra-virgin olive oil

1 medium onion, grated

1 large carrot, peeled and grated

5 garlic cloves, grated

1 (28-ounce) can crushed tomatoes with juice

½ teaspoon dried oregano

Pinch sugar (optional)

Kosher salt

Freshly ground black pepper

1. Preheat the Instant Pot by selecting Sauté.

2. Once hot, add the oil followed by the onion and carrot. Sauté for 2 minutes until the onion is translucent. Add the garlic and cook for 30 seconds.

3. Add the tomatoes with juice and stir. Add the oregano and secure the lid.

4. Select Manual and cook at high pressure for 30 minutes.

5. Once cooking is complete, use a natural release for 10 minutes, then release any remaining pressure.

6. Stir and taste for seasoning. Add the sugar (if using), and season with salt and pepper as desired. Store for up to a week in the refrigerator or freeze for several months.

VARIATION TIP: Add a pinch of red pepper flakes for a little heat, or a sprinkle of basil for freshness.

Per Serving (¾ cup) Calories: 103; Total Carbohydrates: 10g; Saturated Fat: 1g; Trans Fat: 0g; Fiber: 2g; Protein: 2g; Sodium: 350mg

Puttanesca Sauce

GLUTEN-FREE, PALEO-FRIENDLY *Puttanesca is a tomato-based pasta sauce that's briny and tangy, thanks to Kalamata olives, capers, and anchovies. It packs a lot of flavor into a small area, making your next pasta dish the opposite of bland.*

PREP: 10 MINUTES • PRESSURE: 20 MINUTES • TOTAL: 45 MINUTES
PRESSURE LEVEL: HIGH • RELEASE: NATURAL

1. Preheat the Instant Pot by selecting Sauté.

2. Once hot, add the oil followed by the onion. Sauté for 3 minutes, then add the garlic. Sauté 1 minute more.

3. Add the tomatoes with juice, squishing each one with your hand as it goes into the pot. Add the olives, anchovies, tomato paste, capers, and red pepper flakes. Season with salt and pepper. Secure the lid.

4. Select Manual and cook at high pressure for 20 minutes.

5. Once cooking is complete, use a natural release for 10 minutes, then release any remaining pressure. Stir and taste for seasoning.

6. If a thicker sauce is desired, select Sauté and simmer for 5 minutes. Serve over pasta.

COOKING TIP: This recipe makes enough sauce to top 8 ounces of pasta.

Per Serving (1 cup) Calories: 145; Total Carbohydrates: 11g; Saturated Fat: 1g; Trans Fat: 0g; Fiber: 3g; Protein: 4g; Sodium: 806mg

MAKES ABOUT 4 CUPS

2 tablespoons extra-virgin olive oil

1 small onion, finely chopped

4 garlic cloves, minced

1 (28-ounce) can whole tomatoes with juice

½ cup chopped pitted Kalamata olives

4 anchovy fillets, drained and minced

1 tablespoon tomato paste

1 tablespoon drained capers

¼ teaspoon red pepper flakes

Kosher salt

Freshly ground black pepper

Broccoli Pesto

VEGETARIAN, GLUTEN-FREE *Broccoli gives a nutritional boost to zesty pesto, making your pasta dinner a complete meal. Walnuts add protein, olive oil adds good fat, and broccoli adds fiber. This pesto tastes great and is super easy to make. Toss it with the pasta of your choice, or use it as a spread in your next grilled cheese (trust me).*

PREP: 10 MINUTES • PRESSURE: 3 MINUTES • TOTAL: 20 MINUTES
PRESSURE LEVEL: HIGH • RELEASE: QUICK

MAKES ABOUT 2½ CUPS

1 bunch broccoli (about 1 pound), cut into florets (reserve stems for vegetable stock)

3 cups water

⅓ cup toasted walnuts

3 garlic cloves, minced

1 packed cup fresh basil leaves

¼ cup extra-virgin olive oil

2 tablespoons freshly squeezed lemon juice

¼ cup grated Parmesan cheese

Kosher salt

Freshly ground black pepper

1. Add the broccoli and water to the Instant Pot. Secure the lid.

2. Select Manual and cook at high pressure for 3 minutes.

3. Meanwhile, combine the walnuts and garlic in a food processor. Pulse several times until crumbly, but before the walnuts turn to butter.

4. Once cooking is complete, use a quick release. Remove the broccoli (reserving the cooking liquid) and rinse with cold water. Drain well and add to the food processor, along with the basil, oil, and lemon juice.

5. Pulse until well mixed. Add ¼ cup of cooking liquid and the Parmesan, and season with salt and pepper. Process until smooth. Add more cooking liquid as needed.

COOKING TIP: You want the broccoli tender but not mushy. Adjust the cook time based on how large your florets are.

Per Serving (½ cup) Calories: 248; Total Carbohydrates: 10g; Saturated Fat: 3g; Trans Fat: 0g; Fiber: 4g; Protein: 9g; Sodium: 144mg

Onion Gravy

You can frequently make a gravy using the juices left over after cooking a hunk of meat in the pressure cooker, but sometimes you need gravy for something like mashed potatoes. This all-purpose gravy gets its deep flavor from browned onions, thyme, and chicken broth. Homemade stock works the best (as always).

PREP: 15 MINUTES • PRESSURE: 10 MINUTES • TOTAL: 40 MINUTES
PRESSURE LEVEL: HIGH • RELEASE: NATURAL

MAKES ABOUT 2½ CUPS

3 tablespoons butter, divided

1 large sweet onion, finely chopped

2 cups chicken broth (try the recipe on page 140)

2 fresh thyme sprigs

1 bay leaf

2 tablespoons all-purpose flour

Kosher salt

Freshly ground black pepper

1. Preheat the Instant Pot by selecting Sauté.

2. Once hot, add 1 tablespoon of butter followed by the onion. Sauté for 6 minutes, until translucent and starting to brown.

3. Add the broth, thyme, and bay leaf. Secure the lid.

4. Select Manual and cook at high pressure for 10 minutes.

5. Once cooking is complete, use a natural release for 10 minutes, then release any remaining pressure.

6. Select Sauté. In a small bowl, knead together the remaining 2 tablespoons of butter with the flour until a pasty ball forms. Add to the simmering broth and stir until the paste is dissolved and the gravy is thick, about 5 minutes.

7. Season with salt and pepper as desired.

INGREDIENT TIP: Cipollini onions, sweet onions, and shallots all work for this recipe.

Per Serving (¼ cup) Calories: 50; Total Carbohydrates: 3g; Saturated Fat: 2g; Trans Fat: 0g; Fiber: 0g; Protein: 1g; Sodium: 193mg

Mango-Apple Chutney

VEGETARIAN, GLUTEN-FREE *Mango chutney is a popular condiment in Indian cuisine and adds sweet and spicy flavor to curries, roasted meats, and more. Here, apples add some extra sweetness and a smooth texture without taking away from the mango taste. The chutney will keep in the refrigerator for up to a month, and can be canned or frozen for up to a year.*

PREP: 10 MINUTES • PRESSURE: 7 MINUTES • TOTAL: 35 MINUTES
PRESSURE LEVEL: HIGH • RELEASE: NATURAL

MAKES ABOUT 3 CUPS

1 tablespoon canola oil

1 large red onion, finely chopped

1 heaping tablespoon grated fresh ginger

1 red Thai chile, cut into a few pieces (optional)

2 large mangos, peeled and diced

2 apples, cored, partially peeled, and diced

1 red bell pepper, diced

½ cup golden raisins

1¼ cups sugar

½ cup apple cider vinegar

1 teaspoon kosher salt

1½ teaspoons curry powder

½ teaspoon ground cinnamon

1 tablespoon freshly squeezed lemon juice

1. Preheat the Instant Pot by selecting Sauté. Add the oil.

2. Once hot, add the onion and sauté for 3 minutes. Add the ginger and chile (if using), and cook for 1 minute.

3. Add the mangos, apples, bell pepper, raisins, sugar, vinegar, salt, curry powder, and cinnamon. Secure the lid.

4. Select Manual and cook at high pressure for 7 minutes.

5. Once cooking is complete, use a natural release for 10 minutes, then release any remaining pressure.

6. Select Sauté and simmer the sauce until thickened, stirring occasionally, about 10 minutes.

7. Add the lemon juice and stir. Store in airtight containers in the refrigerator for up to a month or in the freezer for up to a year.

INGREDIENT TIP: It's best to use ripe mangos for this recipe. You can tell if a mango is ripe by squeezing it—if it gives slightly, it's ripe.

Per Serving (¼ cup) Calories: 160; Total Carbohydrates: 38g; Saturated Fat: 0g; Trans Fat: 0g; Fiber: 2g; Protein: 1g; Sodium: 197mg

Cranberry Sauce

VEGETARIAN, GLUTEN-FREE *The holidays just wouldn't be the holidays without cranberry sauce, and this homemade version is on a whole different level than the canned stuff. It's tart, sweet, and a bit spicy thanks to a dose of ginger. Because cranberries are so acidic, this sauce will keep for up to three weeks in the refrigerator.*

PREP: 5 MINUTES • PRESSURE: 15 MINUTES • TOTAL: 35 MINUTES
PRESSURE LEVEL: HIGH • RELEASE: NATURAL

MAKES ABOUT 2 CUPS

4 cups washed cranberries, fresh or frozen

1 (1-inch) piece ginger, peeled and cut into ⅛-inch slices

½ cup freshly squeezed orange juice

Zest from ½ orange

Juice and zest from ½ lemon

1 cup sugar

1. Add the cranberries, ginger, orange juice, orange zest, lemon juice, lemon zest, and sugar to the Instant Pot. Secure the lid.

2. Select Manual and cook at high pressure for 15 minutes.

3. Once cooking is complete, use a natural release for 10 minutes, then release any remaining pressure.

4. Let cool and remove the ginger if desired. The liquid will thicken as it cools. The sauce will keep in the refrigerator for up to 3 weeks.

INGREDIENT TIP: Be sure to pick through your cranberries and remove any shriveled or bad-looking ones before cooking.

Per Serving (⅓ cup) Calories: 177; Total Carbohydrates: 43g; Saturated Fat: 0g; Trans Fat: 0g; Fiber: 3g; Protein: 0g; Sodium: 0mg

Cinnamon Applesauce

VEGETARIAN, GLUTEN-FREE, PALEO-FRIENDLY *I always make a big batch of homemade applesauce at the end of apple season. I tend to go a bit overboard buying apples, and applesauce is an easy but delicious way to enjoy the remaining fruits. Even mushy apples will taste great once they're cooked into this naturally sweet sauce.*

PREP: 15 MINUTES • PRESSURE: 4 MINUTES • TOTAL: 30 MINUTES
PRESSURE LEVEL: HIGH • RELEASE: NATURAL

MAKES ABOUT 4 CUPS

10 to 12 medium apples, peeled, cored, and roughly diced

½ cup apple cider, apple juice, or water

1 cinnamon stick, broken in half

Up to ¼ cup honey (optional)

1 tablespoon freshly squeezed lemon juice (optional)

1. Add the apples, cider or juice or water, and both halves of the cinnamon stick to the Instant Pot. Secure the lid.

2. Select Manual and cook at high pressure for 4 minutes.

3. Once cooking is complete, use a natural release.

4. Stir and remove the cinnamon stick halves. If the applesauce isn't sweet enough, add honey. If it isn't tart enough, add lemon juice. If a super smooth texture is desired, use an immersion blender.

COOKING TIP: If you own a food mill, you don't have to peel your apples. Roughly dice them and throw them in the pot with the other ingredients. Once the cooking is done, run the mixture through the food mill.

Per Serving (1 cup) Calories: 237; Total Carbohydrates: 63g; Saturated Fat: 0g; Trans Fat: 0g; Fiber: 11g; Protein: 1g; Sodium: 5mg

Orange and Lemon Marmalade

VEGETARIAN, GLUTEN-FREE *By combining oranges and lemons, this marmalade is not too bitter and not too sweet. The citrusy spread comes together easily in the pressure cooker and can be stored in the refrigerator or canned for longer storage. Displayed in a pretty jar and labeled, it makes a lovely gift.*

PREP: 15 MINUTES • PRESSURE: 14 MINUTES • TOTAL: 45 MINUTES
PRESSURE LEVEL: HIGH • RELEASE: NATURAL

MAKES 6 CUPS

1½ pounds sweet oranges

8 ounces lemons, such as Meyer lemons

1 cup water

3 pounds sugar

1. Cut the oranges and lemons into ⅛-inch slices (a mandoline comes in handy here). Discard the end pieces that are all peel or pith, and remove the seeds and set aside for use later. Cut the slices into 4 or 5 pieces.

2. Add the fruit and water to the Instant Pot. Secure the lid.

3. Select Manual and cook at high pressure for 14 minutes.

4. Once cooking is complete, use a natural release. Add the sugar and stir until dissolved. Place the seeds in a tea bag or gauze packet, cinch, and place in the mixture. Taste for sweetness.

5. Select Sauté on high heat and boil for about 5 minutes, or until the marmalade sets. This will register as about 220°F on a thermometer. Remove the seed packet and discard.

6. Pour into clean jars and let them sit at room temperature until totally cooled. Store in jars in the refrigerator for up to 3 weeks or the freezer for several months. Alternatively, the marmalade can be canned and kept for a year.

VARIATION TIP: Make this an all-lemon marmalade and increase the sugar to 4 pounds, or make it an all-orange marmalade and decrease the sugar to 2 to 2½ pounds.

Per Serving (2 tablespoons) Calories: 114; Total Carbohydrates: 31g; Saturated Fat: 0g; Trans Fat: 0g; Fiber: 0g; Protein: 0g; Sodium: 0mg

Triple-Berry Jam

VEGETARIAN, GLUTEN-FREE *The Instant Pot turns fresh berries into a not-too-sweet and lively jam in no time. Add more or less of each berry as you see fit, just as long as the total weight is the same. You may need to adjust the amount of sugar depending on how sweet your berries are.*

PREP: 5 MINUTES • PRESSURE: 8 MINUTES • TOTAL: 45 MINUTES
PRESSURE LEVEL: HIGH • RELEASE: NATURAL

MAKES ABOUT 2 CUPS

8 ounces fresh strawberries, hulled and halved

8 ounces fresh blueberries

8 ounces fresh raspberries

1 cup sugar

2 teaspoons freshly squeezed lemon juice

1 teaspoon grated lemon zest

Up to ¼ cup honey (optional)

1. Add the strawberries, blueberries, raspberries, and sugar to the Instant Pot and stir. Let it sit for at least 15 minutes or up to 1 hour.

2. Select Sauté and bring the mixture to a boil for 3 minutes. Secure the lid.

3. Select Manual and cook at high pressure for 8 minutes.

4. Once cooking is complete, use a natural release. This will take about 10 minutes.

5. Remove the lid and select Sauté. Add the lemon juice and zest. Carefully taste the jam (it's hot!) and add honey if needed. Boil for 3 to 4 minutes, stirring frequently, or until the gel point is reached. This will register as 220°F on a thermometer, and will coat the back of a wooden spoon.

6. Select Cancel. Mash the jam if a smoother texture is desired. Carefully transfer to lidded containers, close, and let them cool. The jam will keep in the refrigerator for up to 3 weeks or the freezer for at least 6 months.

COOKING TIP: If you like a really smooth, seedless jam, push the fruit through a strainer between steps 4 and 5, then proceed with the recipe as written. Be careful, since the fruit will be hot.

Per Serving (¼ cup) Calories: 134; Total Carbohydrates: 35g; Saturated Fat: 0g; Trans Fat: 0g; Fiber: 3g; Protein: 1g; Sodium: 1mg

Apple Butter

VEGETARIAN, GLUTEN-FREE *The pressure cooker makes homemade apple butter a largely hands-off affair. The apples cook until very tender and are then simmered with brown sugar until thick. Slather on a hot biscuit or scone, or give as a thoughtful gift.*

PREP: 10 MINUTES • PRESSURE: 30 MINUTES • TOTAL: 1 HOUR, 30 MINUTES • PRESSURE LEVEL: HIGH • RELEASE: NATURAL

MAKES ABOUT 2 CUPS

4 pounds apples, peeled, cored, and roughly chopped

½ cup apple cider

1 tablespoon freshly squeezed lemon juice

1 cup brown sugar

1 teaspoon ground cinnamon

Pinch ground cloves or nutmeg

Pinch kosher salt

1. Add the apples and cider to the Instant Pot. Secure the lid.

2. Select Manual and cook at high pressure for 30 minutes.

3. Once cooking is complete, use a natural release. This will take about 15 minutes.

4. Add the lemon juice, brown sugar, cinnamon, cloves or nutmeg, and salt and stir. Select Sauté and cook, stirring occasionally, for about 30 minutes, or until thickened and a deep amber color.

5. Store in an airtight container in the refrigerator for up to a week or in the freezer for up to 3 months.

INGREDIENT TIP: Use a mix of different apples for the best flavor.

Per Serving (¼ cup) Calories: 195; Total Carbohydrates: 51g; Saturated Fat: 0g; Trans Fat: 0g; Fiber: 6g; Protein: 1g; Sodium: 27mg

ELECTRIC PRESSURE COOKING TIME CHARTS

The following charts provide approximate cooking times for a variety of foods using the Instant Pot. Slightly different ingredients, sizes, liquids, prep, and more can affect the cook time, so consider this a starting point.

BEANS AND LEGUMES

When cooking beans, always include a dose of oil to reduce foaming and use a natural release. Your cook time will vary depending upon the age of your beans—old beans take longer to soften.

| | MINUTES UNDER PRESSURE: | | PRESSURE | RELEASE |
	SOAKED	UNSOAKED		
BLACK BEANS	10 to 15	22 to 27	High	Natural
BLACK-EYED PEAS	5 to 10	10 to 15	High	Natural
CANNELLINI BEANS	10 to 15	30 to 35	High	Natural
CHICKPEAS (GARBANZO BEANS)	15 to 20	35 to 40	High	Natural
KIDNEY BEANS	10 to 15	25 to 30	High	Natural
LENTILS	——	12 to 17	High	Natural
NAVY BEANS	10 to 15	20 to 25	High	Natural
PINTO BEANS	10 to 15	25 to 30	High	Natural
SOYBEANS, DRIED	20 to 25	30 to 35	High	Natural
SPLIT PEAS	——	5 to 10	High	Natural

GRAINS

To prevent foaming, add a small amount of oil or butter to the pot.
Rinsing your grains before cooking also helps.

	LIQUID PER 1 CUP OF GRAINS	MINUTES UNDER PRESSURE	PRESSURE	RELEASE
ARBORIO AND CALROSE RICE	2 cups	6 to 7	High	Quick
BARLEY, PEARLED	3 cups	20 to 25	High	Natural
BARLEY, WHOLE-GRAIN	3 cups	30 to 35	High	Natural
BROWN RICE, LONG-GRAIN	1¼ cups	20 to 24	High	Natural for 10 minutes, then quick
BULGUR	3 cups	8 to 10	High	Natural
FARRO, SEMI-PEARLED	2½ cups	10 to 12	High	Natural
OATS, ROLLED	2 cups	5	High	Natural for 10 minutes, then quick
OATS, STEEL-CUT	3 cups	5 to 10	High	Natural
QUINOA	2 cups	1 to 2	High	Natural for 10 minutes, then quick
WHITE RICE, LONG-GRAIN	1½ cups	4	High	Natural for 10 minutes, then quick
WILD RICE	3 cups	25	High	Natural for 10 minutes, then quick

MEAT

Consult your recipe of choice for more exact cooking times to prevent undercooking or overcooking your meat.

	MINUTES UNDER PRESSURE	PRESSURE	RELEASE
BEEF BONE-IN SHORT RIBS	35 to 45	High	Natural or quick
BEEF BRISKET	60 to 90	High	Natural
BEEF ROUND, RUMP, OR POT ROAST	40 to 70	High	Natural
BEEF, STEW MEAT (CUBED)	15 to 20	High	Natural or quick
LAMB CHOPS	5 to 10	High	Quick
LAMB, CUBED	10 to 15	High	Quick
LAMB, GROUND	8 to 15	High	Quick
PORK BABY BACK RIBS	25 to 30	High	Natural
PORK CHOPS	6 to 10	High	Quick
PORK, CUBED	10 to 20	High	Quick
PORK LOIN	15 to 25	High	Natural
PORK SAUSAGE (RAW)	8 to 11	High	Natural
PORK SHOULDER OR BUTT ROAST	45 to 60	High	Natural

POULTRY

Consult your recipe of choice for more exact cooking times to prevent undercooking or overcooking poultry.

	MINUTES UNDER PRESSURE	PRESSURE	RELEASE
CHICKEN BREAST, BONE-IN	7 to 10	High	Quick or natural
CHICKEN BREAST, BONELESS	5 to 8	High	Quick
CHICKEN THIGH, BONE-IN	10 to 15	High	Natural
CHICKEN WINGS	10 to 12	High	Quick
DUCK QUARTERS, BONE-IN	10 to 20	High	Quick
TURKEY BREAST, BONELESS	15 to 20	High	Natural
TURKEY, GROUND	8 to 10	High	Quick or natural

SEAFOOD

Seafood is easily overcooked in the Instant Pot, so be conservative with your cook times. You can always add cook time if needed.

	MINUTES UNDER PRESSURE	PRESSURE	RELEASE
COD OR TILAPIA	3 to 5	Low	Quick
CRAB	3 to 5	Low	Quick
HALIBUT	6 to 7	Low	Quick
MUSSELS	2 to 3	Low	Quick
SALMON	5 to 7	Low	Quick
SHRIMP	3 to 6	Low	Quick

VEGETABLES

Vegetable cooking times will vary depending on the size, whether they are being steamed or cooked in liquid, and more.

	MINUTES UNDER PRESSURE	PRESSURE	RELEASE
ARTICHOKES, MEDIUM, WHOLE	11 to 14	High	Natural
BEETS, MEDIUM, WHOLE	15 to 20	High	Quick
BRUSSELS SPROUTS, WHOLE	3 to 5	High	Quick
BUTTERNUT SQUASH, 1-INCH CHUNKS	4 to 6	High	Quick
CABBAGE, SLICED	3 to 5	High	Quick
CARROTS, 1-INCH PIECES	2 to 4	High	Quick
CORN ON THE COB	4	High	Quick
GREEN BEANS	2 to 4	High	Quick
POTATOES, 1-INCH CHUNKS	4 to 7	High	Natural
POTATOES, BABY	5 to 10	High	Natural
SPAGHETTI SQUASH, HALVED	5 to 10	High	Quick
SWEET POTATOES, MEDIUM, WHOLE	10 to 15	High	Quick
TOMATOES, CUT UP FOR SAUCE	5 to 7	High	Natural

THE DIRTY DOZEN
AND THE CLEAN FIFTEEN

A nonprofit and environmental watchdog organization called the Environmental Working Group (EWG) looks at data supplied by the US Department of Agriculture (USDA) and the Food and Drug Administration (FDA) about pesticide residues. Each year it compiles a list of the lowest and highest pesticide loads found in commercial crops. You can use these lists to decide which fruits and vegetables to buy organic to minimize your exposure to pesticides and which produce is considered safe enough to buy conventionally. This does not mean they are pesticide-free, though, so wash these fruits and vegetables thoroughly.

These lists change every year, so make sure you look up the most recent one before you fill your shopping cart. You'll find the most recent lists as well as a guide to pesticides in produce at EWG.org/FoodNews.

The Dirty Dozen	The Clean Fifteen
Apples	Asparagus
Celery	Avocados
Cherry tomatoes	Cabbage
Cucumbers	Cantaloupes (domestic)
Grapes	Cauliflower
Nectarines (imported)	Eggplants
Peaches	Grapefruits
Potatoes	Kiwis
Snap peas (imported)	Mangos
Spinach	Onions
Strawberries	Papayas
Sweet bell peppers	Pineapples
	Sweet corn
* Kale/Collard greens	Sweet peas (frozen)
Hot peppers	Sweet potatoes

* In addition to the dirty dozen, the EWG added two produce contaminated with highly toxic organo-phosphate insecticides.

CONVERSION TABLES

VOLUME EQUIVALENTS (LIQUID)

US STANDARD	US STANDARD (OUNCES)	METRIC (APPROXIMATE)
2 tablespoons	1 fl. oz.	30 mL
¼ cup	2 fl. oz.	60 mL
½ cup	4 fl. oz.	120 mL
1 cup	8 fl. oz.	240 mL
1½ cups	12 fl. oz.	355 mL
2 cups or 1 pint	16 fl. oz.	475 mL
4 cups or 1 quart	32 fl. oz.	1 L
1 gallon	128 fl. oz.	4 L

OVEN TEMPERATURES

FAHRENHEIT (F)	CELSIUS (C) (APPROXIMATE)
250°F	120°C
300°F	150°C
325°F	165°C
350°F	180°C
375°F	190°C
400°F	200°C
425°F	220°C
450°F	230°C

VOLUME EQUIVALENTS (DRY)

US STANDARD	METRIC (APPROXIMATE)
¼ teaspoon	1 mL
½ teaspoon	2 mL
1 teaspoon	5 mL
1 tablespoon	15 mL
¼ cup	59 mL
⅓ cup	79 mL
½ cup	118 mL
1 cup	177 mL

WEIGHT EQUIVALENTS

US STANDARD	METRIC (APPROXIMATE)
½ ounce	15 g
1 ounce	30 g
2 ounces	60 g
4 ounces	115 g
8 ounces	225 g
12 ounces	340 g
16 ounces or 1 pound	455 g

RESOURCES

- The Instant Pot website has more information about the device, recipes, and FAQs: InstantPot.com

- If you've lost your manual, download it from the Instant Pot website: InstantPot.com/benefits/specifications-and-manuals

- Laura Pazzaglia runs a pressure cooker website with recipes, how-tos, and an impressive cook time chart: HipPressureCooking.com

- Lorna Sass is the queen of pressure cooking, and has written several cookbooks on the subject. Some of her recipes are posted for free on her website: LornaSass.com

- If you want to get experimental with your pressure cooking, consult Modernist Cuisine and their progressive recipes: ModernistCuisine.com

- Jill Nussinow, aka The Veggie Queen, has written a couple of books about vegan pressure cooking and posts recipes on her website: TheVeggieQueen.com

- New electric pressure cooker recipes go up weekly on the Pressure Cooking Today website, with a wide range of dishes and ingredients: PressureCookingToday.com

RECIPE INDEX

INDEX

ABOUT THE AUTHOR

Laurel Randolph is a Los Angeles-based food writer and recipe developer who has contributed food articles to *Paste Magazine, Wise Bread*, and Serious Eats. In her free time, you can usually find her browsing a farmers' market, eating tacos or Vietnamese food, or cooking up a storm at home. Learn more at laurelrandolph.com.

CPSIA information can be obtained
at www.ICGtesting.com
Printed in the USA
BVOW10s1655291017

498842BV00001BC/1/P